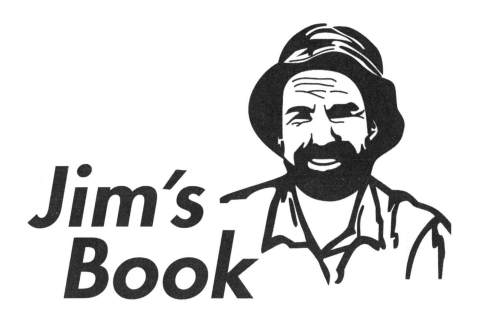

Jim's Book

T0324313

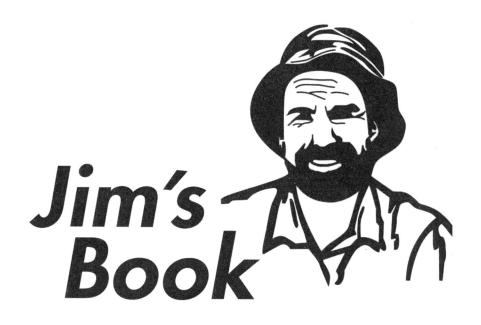

Jim's Book

The Surprising Story of
JIM PENMAN
Australia's Backyard Millionaire

Catherine Moolenschot

WILEY

First published in 2019 by John Wiley & Sons Australia, Ltd
42 McDougall St, Milton Qld 4064

Office also in Melbourne

Typeset in Garamond Premier Pro 12.5/18pt

© Catherine Moolenschot 2019

The moral rights of the author have been asserted

 A catalogue record for this book is available from the National Library of Australia

Cover design by Brio Books Pty Ltd

Printed in Singapore by C.O.S. Printers Pte Ltd

10 9 8 7 6 5 4 3 2 1

Disclaimer
The material in this publication is of the nature of general comment only, and does not represent professional advice. It is not intended to provide specific guidance for particular circumstances and it should not be relied on as the basis for any decision to take action or not take action on any matter which it covers. Readers should obtain professional advice where appropriate, before making any such decision. To the maximum extent permitted by law, the author and publisher disclaim all responsibility and liability to any person, arising directly or indirectly from any person taking or not taking action based on the information in this publication.

Contents

Prologue

I met Jim Penman in September 2017 at a business event held at Foothills Conference Centre, which he owns. A friend had called to offer me a free ticket to the event, adding, 'Jim Penman will be one of the keynote speakers; it'll be a great day'.

'Jim who?' I replied.

'Penman — you know Jim's Mowing? The guy who started it.'

'Oh *Jim*!' Of course I knew of Jim's. Who didn't?

At the event Jim shared the story of his franchise, especially his obsession with great customer service. It was inspiring. He also made a brief mention of his research into the rise and fall of civilisations, which I found fascinating: what can we learn from our past mistakes and successes as a civilisation?

After the talk a small group of us chased Jim down, catching him just before he left for his next appointment. He was happy to chat for five minutes, and gave us all a free copy of his book *Biohistory: The decline and fall of the West* — and, amazingly, his email address.

I love talking with individuals who have achieved a lot, learning valuable insights and hearing their incredible stories, so this was an opportunity I couldn't pass up. I emailed him that night thanking him for the book and suggesting we catch up. He agreed, as he wanted to discuss with me how he could get more exposure for his research, and suggested I read the book first.

I read it over the next month, emailed him, and arranged to meet at Jim's national office. Upon arrival I had two distinct impressions. The first was how beautiful the 20-acre property that hosts Jim's national office and the Foothills Conference Centre is. The second was how unassuming the office buildings are. There was no grand entrance. In fact, the buildings looked rather plain: the main office building is long, and looked from the outside more like a row of schoolrooms than an office. I had a hard time figuring out where to enter until I noticed a laminated sign blue-tacked to one of the doors that read 'National Office'. Surprised, I opened it and stepped into a basic, well-lit, open-plan office.

Valerie Lobo, Jim's employee of over twenty years, pointed me to Jim's office. The door was ajar, and inside he was sitting on a bright-purple exercise ball, working at his computer. I noticed a very basic desk, empty except for his computer. The walls were bare and there was no clutter: no papers, pens, keys or phone, no photos in frames, nothing personal. (Months later I walked into his home office and discovered the walls covered with artwork from his kids, photos of his wife and children, and all the usual desk clutter. It was clear he kept home life and work life separate.)

Jim stood to greet me, immediately launching into a rapid monologue. 'Oh hi there Catherine; I watched your TED talk and it was good. I liked your Funnel of Greatness idea. It's similar to what I say about the importance of character. You seem to be a lively person who communicates well — maybe there is something we can do together.'

Through our chat that day, and more in the following weeks, we arrived at the idea of me writing a biography of Jim, incorporating the differing perspectives of the people who know Jim — 'warts and all', in Jim's words. 'I'm not always easy to work with. I'll introduce you to family, friends, staff, franchisees, franchisors, particularly those who don't like me, so you can have an honest account.'

Throughout my research, Jim has been true to his word. For example, in an email he sent me in April 2018, he suggested I speak with one man in particular: 'He's just launched a legal action and known me for years, so would be a strong negative voice'. He included his email address so I could contact him.

He was also happy to draft and sign a legal document for a number of interviewees who requested it, promising not to sue them for anything they told me.

Jim has given me access to his family, and current and former staff, franchisors and franchisees. I've attended Jim's Group training, staff lunches and Jim's National Conference. I have been to his home and his farm, and have interviewed over one hundred people from all areas of his life. A few have wished to remain anonymous, and a few declined point-blank to be interviewed.

It would have been impossible to include the perspectives of every one of the over 8000 people who have been involved in the Jim's Group over the years, and there have even been too many GMs, COOs and CEOs to adequately cover in one book. Likewise, the expansion into each new Jim's division has not been covered, as that is too long a list; today there are over fifty divisions, plus others that have failed.

My aim is to give you a full account of Jim's life — his character, his business, and his passions — as well as the company's progression over the years. Some people have very different accounts of what happened, and I have done my best to reconcile them.

This book is the story of the unique man who has built the largest home-service franchise in Australia through his passion for franchisees and customers. Yet while this unrelenting passion has driven his business forward over the past thirty years, his temper, unorthodox communication style, and some of his business decisions have put many offside. His story is inspiring, often surprising, and at times very strange.

Summary of the Jim's Group structure

In the beginning the structure was simple, with Jim as the franchisor selling franchises and no layers of management in between. Today, the Jim's Group franchise system is set up as follows.

FRANCHISEES

Franchisees are people who have bought a Jim's franchise and are out mowing lawns, cleaning houses, and so forth. They have a territory that can range from a few hundred households to several postcodes, where they have right of first refusal for all new leads. They can advertise freely within their territory, though most don't do this because joint marketing normally provides all the work they need.

FRANCHISORS

Franchisors are people who look after the franchisees in a certain region. They recruit them and provide ongoing support, such as meetings and phone calls, while managing the advertising for the region. Some franchisors also work in the field themselves as a franchisee.

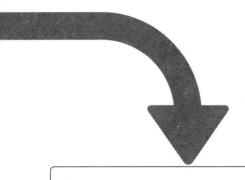

DIVISIONALS

Divisionals look after a division, such as dog wash, antennas, fencing, and so on. They are the first line of support for franchisors and handle the technical aspects of each division, such as up-front training, divisional manuals, and so on. Jim's Group itself is the divisional for thirteen divisions (as of writing), including Mowing.

THE NATIONAL FRANCHISOR

The **National Franchisor**, also known as **Jim's Group** or **National Office**, is Jim's company. It provides support at every level with a particular focus on customer service, support for franchisees, and contracts. Jim Penman is the founder and sole director of Jim's Group.

Introduction: 'The Real Jim'

In the late 1980s Jim Penman was in an 'utter panic'. He had been mowing lawns in Melbourne, employing subcontractors, and selling his excess clients in batches called 'mowing rounds' to people who wanted to start independent mowing businesses. He knew there was a mowing franchise system called VIP in Adelaide that was very successful, but Jim couldn't see how to make a franchise work in a way that would clearly benefit the franchisee.

Then VIP expanded to Victoria and Jim feared they would swallow his entire business. He talked to VIP's Victorian state manager at the time and offered to sell his entire output of mowing clients to VIP on an ongoing basis, making Jim an appendage of VIP. But VIP was a big business that was growing steadily, and the offer was refused. Still, the success of VIP suggested to Jim that franchising was feasible.

Shortly thereafter Jim attended a meeting at his church. That day the talk was about goal-setting, and, as Jim recalled, 'On the spot, I decided that franchising the business would be my goal'.

His first move was to attend the 1988 Melbourne Franchise Show, immediately hiding his nametag upon arrival. He walked straight to the VIP stand and enquired. 'The man gave me a brochure and a long and detailed explanation of the VIP system,' Jim recalled with a grin. After twenty minutes VIP's Victorian state manager arrived, saw Jim, and called out, 'That's Jim Penman! Don't tell him another thing!' But Jim had already learned what he needed to know.

Jim discovered that VIP concentrated work in one area to reduce franchisee travel, provided discounts on equipment and insurance, and allowed franchisees to make extra cash by selling surplus jobs. Plus, if they were sick or injured they could have someone look after their customers, a major concern for contractors. Jim could finally see why franchisees would pay fees for these benefits, but more importantly Jim was, in his words, 'very motivated by defence and survival'.

Jim engaged a solicitor to draw up a franchise agreement, rejecting VIP's, which he considered 'simply unfair to franchisees'. The first thing the solicitor did was create a template for two contracts, one for each company: Jim's Mowing (Australia), and Jim's Mowing (Victoria). 'I said, "What's this for?" and he said, "In case you want to set up interstate". I just laughed,' Jim recalled. His ambition was to survive VIP's expansion to Victoria; he would never get big enough to expand. Still, he ended up agreeing, 'just in case'.

After nine months of arguing over an agreement that the solicitor feared was overly favourable to the franchisee, Jim finally had a franchise agreement he found satisfactory. Though the contract was radically pro-franchisee in many ways, it was still tough on customer service, on-time payment of fees, and that franchisees must always wear their uniform when working.

And so, in June 1989, at the start of a Melbourne winter, Jim Penman launched Jim's Mowing and signed his first franchisee.

Fast forward to today and the Jim's Group is Australia's largest home service franchise, with fifty-two divisions (as of writing — it's rising fast), and with almost 4000 franchisees servicing roughly 35 000 customers a day, on average. The *Australian Financial Review*[1] described the Jim's Group as 'Australia's second-largest franchise player after Australia Post'. Jim begs to differ. 'There may be more than four thousand post offices in Australia but less than three thousand are licensed. Look it up.'

Every week in Australia some 175 000 people have their needs met by a Jim's franchisee. You could wake up one morning and have your antenna fixed, your dog washed, your bookkeeping done, your lawn mowed, your house cleaned, your windows washed, your devices tested and tagged, your computer cleared of viruses, your home cleared of pests, your car detailed, your pool cleaned and a new fence put up — all by a Jim's service. And this isn't even a quarter of what Jim's people do.

Today, the Jim's franchise as a whole turns over roughly half a billion dollars a year. Jim himself employs roughly forty people, and rising. And though franchise numbers have been growing steadily, client demand has risen even faster. In 2016 the Jim's Group turned down 121 000 jobs because there were not enough franchisees to do the work. In 2017 and 2018, the number of 'unserviced leads', as they are called, was 170 000 and 175 000, respectively.

So who is this Jim?

An Aussie icon

What is the first name of the founder of Jim's Mowing? When Jim posed this question to me I made the obvious guess, 'James', as did most of the people I have since asked. Jim shook his head, grinning. 'My first name is David,' he said. I was somewhat dubious so he pulled out his driver's licence to prove it, and, sure enough, it reads 'David J Penman'. 'If you talk to any of my relatives they still call me David,' he laughed.

He started calling himself Jim, he explained, when he worked on a farm after graduating high school. The owner's son was also named David, so he told everyone to call him Jim, from his middle name, James. The new name stuck, and we don't have to contemplate a world serviced by 'David's Mowing'.

Jim has quite a reputation. While writing this book, when it came up in conversation what I was writing, I received an interesting array of responses:

'Oh, Jim! I've heard he's a prick.'

'Man there's a Jim's *everything* these days. Where will they stop? Jim's Haircuts?'

'I heard Jim fired his sister, is it true?'

'I know someone who was a franchisee but left because of all the changes to the contracts.'

'I was a Jim's Mowing guy a number of years ago! I was much fitter back then, of course.'

'Wow — he's an Aussie icon!'

'I've heard some bad things about him.'

Jim Penman is a powerful man with tight control over his franchise system. He is relentless about delivering great customer service and looking after franchisees. He has a rigorous complaint system that he personally manages. Because of his forceful reputation in the business world, I did a double take when I saw him affectionately cuddle, kiss, and tickle his eight-year-old son. I have watched Jim command a room with riddles, jokes and party tricks at a franchisor dinner, and I have had him finish many of our interviews by simply standing up and walking away without saying 'goodbye'.

The first staff member I interviewed wrote me an email beforehand, to give me an initial insight into Jim. Remarkably, Jim was copied into the email, which either shows this employee's extreme confidence in their ability to hold their job, or it shows that Jim doesn't mind his employees being brutally honest with him. Maybe it's both?

> My first direct experience with Jim, beyond the initial 'welcome aboard' handshake, was fear. He was asking me about an ETA on the project that I'd been hired to work on. I told him my estimate and — holy crap — that look in his eyes ... you feel like you're standing on very, very thin ice. I've heard the same about that penetrating stare from other people (who actually did end up getting fired!) ...

> I've got a ton of respect for him. Respect has roots in both admiration and fear, and I have both for Jim ...

> When it comes to business: he's ruthless. If you're not contributing, you're gone. Regardless of your situation. I've seen him fire a guy who was a week from his first baby.

Some of Jim's staff are daunted by him, but not those who communicate with him most. Where other employees see him as domineering, to them he is a passionate, intelligent, 'tough but fair' boss.

In 2012 you might have seen Jim's sister Gill Moxham talk on *Today Tonight* about her own brother firing her. 'The *Today Tonight* interview twisted it,' Gill told me. 'They made it out like it was a family business. They didn't push the fact that Jim shafted me so much.' Needless to say, Gill is still very hurt and mad at him. You'll hear the details of what happened later.

Jim has many contradictions. He is not a likable, social personality, nor is he someone you meet and instantly feel warmth for. Yet he has a lot of people in his life, gets on well with his kids, has been married to his current wife for seventeen years, and has friends he sees weekly. Jim is known to change his mind often, make decisions very quickly and get angry in an instant. ('Of the seven sins, wrath is definitely my downfall,' Jim admitted.)

Jim responds to emails with record speed, though often without thinking through how his response will sound to the recipient. And he doesn't add niceties like 'Hi Catherine, I hope you're well' to his emails; he is famous for replying abruptly. Jim has a reputation of being a firer, with many franchisors laughing that 'it's always a revolving door at National Office'. And yet he has multiple staff members who have worked for him for five to ten years, and some who have been there for over twenty.

Jim is generally seen as ruthless and tough in business, not one to be crossed lightly. And yet the Jim's Group has avoided litigation better than most franchise systems. Though himself a powerful and forceful man, he believes passionately in the rights of the underdog, which is why his contracts are unique in allowing franchisees to vote out franchisors who do not support them properly, and in allowing franchisees to walk away and operate independently.

Jim is the easiest person to reach that I have ever met. He gives all franchisees his direct phone number and email address and actively encourages them to contact him at any time, responding with lightning speed when they do. Yet he has many faults as a manager, which he admits openly. Many of his staff, franchisors and franchisees say he doesn't know how to manage anything effectively, and yet, somehow, he has built an enterprise that has far outstripped its competitors. Though Jim is deeply and ferociously ambitious, he lives a simple lifestyle and pours every dollar he can into finding a cure for addiction, depression and other ills.

So among all of this — who is Jim, really?

And how on earth did he build Australia's (if not the world's) most successful home-service franchise?

Is he a tyrant? Or a saint?

1

The Early Years

Jim's father, Tom Penman, was a product of his British upbringing. Tom's father had been a senior manager for an electricity company and his great-grandfather David Penman, Jim's great-great-grandfather, was a sea captain who went down in a storm in the Bay of Biscay. He had become a family legend and Jim's personal hero, as someone who had risen from poverty to success. Jim's mother, Margaret Moxham, was one of six children growing up in Scone, a small country town roughly 250 kilometres north of Sydney. Margaret's father was a shire clerk. Both of Jim's parents came from upper-middle-class, educated families.

Jim's mother was a maverick for her time. She was denied enlistment for World War II since primary teaching was a reserved occupation. But as soon as the war ended she used her savings to buy a ticket on the first civilian ship allowed into the UK after the war. Once on English soil she hitchhiked from place to place, having the time of her life. This was in the late 1940s, when women just didn't do that kind of thing.

At a youth hostel in Wales Margaret met an Englishman, Tom Penman. They courted in Wales before deciding to holiday on the continent together, where they argued the whole time. 'And then they just thought, "We might as well get married". It wasn't romantic in any normal sense,' Jim said. 'Mum chose Dad because he didn't bore her, and she thought she wouldn't find anyone better.'

They settled in Halesowen, Worcestershire, and soon had their first child, Lynne, after which Margaret became severely depressed but received no support. 'What we see now as post-natal depression, the doctors saw then as a madwoman,' Jim's sister Gill said. The doctors simply gave Margaret Valium, which gave her bad side effects, so they gave her other tablets to help. Unfortunately those tablets also had side effects.

'She was on about twenty-five tablets a day for thirty-three years,' Gill said.

> Every time she got pregnant she would stop having the tablets, cold turkey, because even she was aware — with the knowledge at that time — that they could affect the child. I don't know if that had any influence on our very early gestation, who can tell ...

Despite the fact that, according to Gill, 'Dad was extremely unsupportive when Mum was pregnant', Margaret and Tom went on to have three more children: David (Jim), on 8 May 1952, and two years later another son, Chris. Gill was born five years after Chris. (Lynne and Chris declined to be interviewed for this book.)

In 1955, when Jim was three, Tom became a Ten Pound Pom and the family moved to Australia so Tom could lecture in engineering at Adelaide University. The family moved into a basic commission house in Adelaide.

Margaret was unhappy as a homemaker. 'If she was born later she'd have been a doctor or some sort of highly successful person, but for a woman in the 1950s that wasn't on,' Jim said. 'My mother was loving, but temperamental. She'd lose her temper and we learned to be wary of her moods.' Margaret was anxious and worried a lot, but she was also an intelligent, strong-willed and capable woman. She taught Jim to read before he went to school, and he fondly remembers that she wrote a children's book for him called 'David and the Dinosaurs'.

After a few years the Penmans could afford to buy a red-brick house in Glen Osmond, Adelaide. When Jim was seven his mother gave birth to Gill, and again Margaret suffered severe post-natal depression. There would be a knock on the door in the early hours of the morning, and Tom would answer to find a police officer and his wife on the doorstep.

'Dr Penman, we found your wife wandering the streets,' the police officer would explain.

Tom would reply, 'She's a grown woman, she can do exactly what she wants', showing no concern that her unhappiness drove her out of the house and onto the streets in the middle of the night.

'They should have been married for six months, because that is how long they got on for,' Gill reflected. Jim's view of his father was that he was

> totally traditional in the sense that he didn't like to talk about feelings and thus couldn't relate to Mum that well, but he was totally dedicated to his family ... I can remember him working night and day and living in what today people would consider poverty, so we would have the best start in life. And he clearly loved Mum, even if he couldn't give her what she needed.

Despite Margaret's unhappiness, and despite the drugs clouding her thinking, she was still an amazing mother. 'I loved my mother very much,' Jim said. Gill shared that Margaret 'had the skill to know when a child was ready for a certain book, or to play at maths, or to draw. She was always there for us'.

All the Penman children helped out with chores. Jim remembers doing the dishes, putting mallee roots in the firebox and cleaning out the ash from the fireplace. As a young boy Jim's dream job evolved from train driver to doctor to vet (he found animals easier to get along with than people).

Jim got on well with his brother Chris, and the two of them fought and played together all the time. 'We were a strong pair,' Jim said. 'Chris was my closest friend, and the best man at my first wedding.'

He didn't get on so well with Lynne as a child, though of all the siblings they are closest to each other today. Gill remembers Lynne once saying to her that '"up to the age of about seven he was nice, then all of a sudden he turned into a sour little boy." Now,' Gill added, 'whether that was when his Asperger's kicked in, or me coming along totally unexpectedly was the thing, I'm not sure.'

Gill remembers getting along very well with Jim when she was little.

I thought he was just wonderful…but he gets on with children because they don't have their own opinions. As soon as somebody says something that is opposing to what he thinks, he reacts strongly.

A few moments later Gill, memories perhaps clouded by more recent interactions with Jim, added, 'He's always been an arrogant arsehole, but he takes after Dad'. For his part, Jim said that Gill 'was a cute little girl, I was very fond of her'.

The boys were sent to Prince Alfred College in Adelaide, a school that was founded by the Methodist Church in 1869 and still exists today. Jim recalls that the school was okay, but he has no warm feeling for it: 'I was a solitary kid who got picked on. School was just something to go through.' He wasn't social and didn't bond well with his classmates, instead burying his head in books.

The gardening begins

At eight Jim joined Cub Scouts, though he was not particularly good at it. He didn't get many badges and had few friends. But some good did come of it: cubs were encouraged to do odd jobs around the neighbourhood to earn money for the troop. It was called 'bob-a-job' in those days, because you would get paid a bob (one shilling) for a job. The Penmans knew their neighbour over the back fence, Mr Tapley, quite well, and so eight-year-old Jim knocked on his door. Mr Tapley gave Jim the job of raking his gravel driveway. 'He was a gentleman who never raised his voice in all the years I knew him,' Jim said. It became an ongoing arrangement, with Mr Tapley asking Jim to do the weeding and other simple gardening jobs. 'He paid me two shillings a week,' Jim recalled with glee, 'which was good value then. You could buy a large block of Cadbury chocolate with it, though I didn't buy one often. I was a saver!'

Tom saw Jim's effort in Mr Tapley's garden and figured Jim was now old enough to help out in theirs. They had a push mower, and their backyard was the first lawn Jim ever mowed. It wasn't easy: 'Twigs from the trees were forever jamming the blades, and the backyard was terribly sloped,' Jim said.

Jim soon gained his second client, another friendly, gentlemanly neighbour who lived across the road. He was Polish and had been in a prisoner-of-war camp for Polish officers in World War II. 'He was very kind to me,' Jim remembered.

One day Jim went to Mr Tapley's house to work in the garden as usual, but the gravel drive did not need raking and there was no weeding to be done. 'Why don't you carry that pile of rubbish to the incinerator?' Mr Tapley suggested, and so Jim did.

When he was finished Mr Tapley inspected Jim's work and found leaves and twigs dropped along the way. 'If you're not going to do it properly, I might as well do it myself,' Jim remembered Mr Tapley saying in a sad tone. Jim was filled with deep shame, and a strong determination to never let Mr Tapley down again. This was the moment Jim became obsessed with always doing an outstanding job, and to this day he is obsessive about his franchisees delivering excellent customer service. 'I am notoriously emotional in my attitude to customer service — I feel very upset when any one of my customers has been let down.'

The spark of a lifelong passion

When Jim was ten Tom took the family to England for a year, on study leave with his job as a lecturer at Adelaide University. Tom's work was at an atomic research centre in Berkshire, England, but it left plenty of spare time.

'We spent the whole year driving, looking at castles, cathedrals, Roman roads, searching for flints that might be prehistoric knives,' Jim said animatedly. 'It was quite extraordinary, I remember more of that one year than the whole rest of my childhood.' It fueled his love of history.

Jim's maternal grandfather had died of pneumonia back in Australia before Jim was born, and he didn't see his maternal grandmother often because she lived in Sydney. This trip gave Jim and his siblings time to see their paternal grandparents in England, though it wasn't long enough to build any serious bond. 'They were quite indulgent of us, nothing like what my father experienced as a kid. Dad had an austere upbringing, with few obvious shows of affection,' Jim said.

Jim and his siblings went to school in a twin village called Aston Upthorpe/Aston Tirrold, in Oxfordshire, England. There were only two teachers for the whole primary school: one for years one and two, and another for years three to six. Jim didn't get on well with the other kids, and one day 'a gang of four set on me after school, so I hit one and pushed another over and ran for it,' Jim said. It worked well enough that they didn't try it again.

This village school was the first time Jim was in a co-ed environment, and it was here he had his first crush on a girl. It came to nothing, but Jim still recalls his year in England as 'the most amazing experience. It was quite life-changing'.

The Penmans returned to Adelaide, and the kids to their respective schools. In Jim's first year of high school another boy, Nobbs, 'used to really have a go at me. He just took a dislike for some reason,' Jim said. Nobbs picked on him often, and it got to a point that Jim wanted to leave the school. But one day, when Nobbs balled a scrap of paper and threw it at Jim, Jim exploded. 'I went for him, attacking him,' Jim recalled. They overturned several desks in their fight, and it was quickly big news around the school. 'Even months later boys used to talk about the Nobbs – Penman fight,' Jim chuckled. After that things got easier and he decided to stay.

A significant gift

In 1966, the year Jim turned fourteen, the family moved to Sydney for a year because Tom took a job with Austin Anderson, a consulting firm. The boys went to Sydney Church of England Grammar School,

'Shore' for short, an Anglican all-boys school. In a physical education class they measured their pulse rates and Jim realised he was one of the least fit kids, so he started jogging regularly. 'This was in the 1960s, well before jogging became popular,' Jim said. Today, he still runs almost daily.

As a teenager Jim had begun to hate birthdays and receiving presents, and he still hates them today:

> It's probably got something to do with the fact that, having no social skills whatsoever, if you're given a present you don't really want, you're supposed to make a pleasant comment … but I can't do that. I can't appreciate something I really don't want, I'm unable to pretend.

But, in a contradiction characteristic of Jim, one particular gift changed the course of his life.

Jim made one friend in Sydney, Harold Richards, whose family had a beautiful house on Sydney Harbour. When saying goodbye at the end of the year, Harold gave Jim a present. It was *The Peloponnesian Wars*, an account by Thucydides (460 – 400 BC) of the great struggle between Athens and Sparta, in which Thucydides himself had actually fought. Thucydides took great care with his sources and was keen to understand motivations and root causes, so, although he was Athenian, his account is unusually balanced and he was often critical of his own city.

Thucydides has been called 'the father of scientific history', and this book had a huge impact on Jim. Athens at that time was, in Jim's opinion, perhaps 'the most brilliant city of all time', and he struggled with the question of why Athens declined so quickly, losing its creative brilliance and falling subject to Macedon in just a few decades.

Reading this book triggered an ongoing obsession with the fall of Rome. Not only was it fascinating in its own right, Jim also saw obvious parallels with our own time. 'Even in the 1960s, there was an obvious decline in traditional standards and in religion, just as in the late Roman Republic,' Jim said. He wondered: Was our own civilisation heading the same way as Athens and Rome? And if so, could anything be done about it?

The apple doesn't fall far from the tree

In early 1967 the Penmans moved from Sydney to Melbourne, where Tom had been appointed Chief Engineer at Carlton United Breweries. It was Jim's first time in the city that would become his home. Tom and Margaret could now afford to buy a posh house in North Balwyn.

The boys were sent to Melbourne Grammar, with Jim joining Miller House, and the girls were sent to Presbyterian Ladies' College. Andrew Michelmore attended Melbourne Grammar from Grade 7 and recalls Jim joining his class in 1967.

'David [Jim] was pretty quiet, but he had a strong character,' Andrew recalled.

> I remember there were a couple of arguments, discussions on things, and he didn't back off. I can picture David in an argument about something and reacting very strongly and very quickly. He was this quiet, unassuming guy who went about his own business, and then it was like someone would light a match and wha! That's when you saw the strength of his character.

This quick temper is something staff, franchisors and franchisees were to experience on many occasions.

'Jim was very studious,' Andrew Michelmore added. 'He had a strong underlying character; he is easily underestimated.'

Jolyon Shelton, who was also in Jim's class, remembered that 'David Penman was very smart,' but added that 'he didn't strike me as the really brilliant type, nor a successful businessman. He was quiet and reserved and kept his own company'.

Stewart Niemann, another of Jim's classmates, remembered that Jim 'came across as one of those English types, a bit cultured'. Stewart added that Jim often had 'his nose in books, which was reasonably unusual, to read outside of the curriculum'.

Though Melbourne Grammar was an Anglican school, Jim's questioning mind led him to the conclusion that God didn't exist. 'I was pretty militant, actually. At school I would pin people down and ask whether they believed in God, and argue with them,' Jim said. He and a friend went to a Billy Graham crusade to make fun of the people there. 'So I was kind of anti, you could say,' Jim chuckled. But at the same time he was drawn to Christianity... Whenever someone came to the Penmans' front door, no matter what religion they represented, Tom and Margaret would invite them in; it was the family's way. Said Jim,

> There was something that attracted me [to religion], but I fought against it. Emotionally, it all made pretty good sense. In a way I was saying 'I don't think there is a God. Convince me'.

But he was to remain a militant agnostic for many years to come.

Tom worked at Carlton United Breweries for the next two years, at which point he lost the job due to his inability to get on with (in his words, according to Jim) 'eighteenth-century management'. 'He wasn't tactful enough, just like me,' Jim explained.

Tom went on to launch a successful consulting business, solving murders and investigating fires. One case Jim vividly remembers is that of a young man who crashed his car, killing his fiancée. The police found that he had been drinking heavily and speeding, and the young man was facing several years in prison. The defence lawyer called on Tom to see if there was anything to be done.

Tom assessed the skid marks and showed they were consistent with someone travelling the speed limit. He asked the paramedic, 'Did you swab his skin with alcohol before taking the blood sample?' They responded they had. 'That accounts for the alcohol,' Tom replied. He also pointed out that the man had been having dinner with his future father-in-law who was a Methodist minister, so it was extremely unlikely he had been drinking at all. 'This young man,' Jim said,

> whose life would have been ... I mean, it's bad enough your fiancée gets killed, he would have been destroyed by being sent to jail for culpable driving ... And he gets out, because of my father. Dad was a really brilliant man. Very tactless, with limited social skills and not a great husband. But very driven and smart.

Years later Andrew Michelmore, Jim's former classmate, was working at Conzinc Riotinto Australia, which during a particular case used an expert witness in chemical engineering, 'and it was Tom Penman, David's father!' Andrew recalled. Andrew expected Jim to go on and have a career similar to his father's, 'being an expert in something and providing considered advice,' Andrew said.

Tom Penman was always full of ideas and he encouraged thinking, learning and researching in his children. When the family watched a historical film on television Tom would grab the encyclopaedia and read out what really happened during the commercials. 'As a kid you don't appreciate that,' Jim said.

Despite the respect Jim has today for his father, as a teenager it was a tough relationship.

He was a very conscientious and concerned father, but not exactly a softy. I would never have dreamed of disobeying him! There was a time when I stopped speaking to him entirely. At the dinner table he told me to shut up, probably because I was having a go at him. So, I did, for six months. It was really horrible when I think about it, because my father sacrificed so much for us, and yet he was a pretty fierce character and I fought with him. Later I did thank him for all he had done, but after he died I wished I had apologised to him for being such an ass as a teenager.

Jim's teenage rebellion took a distinct form, however. Rather than indulging in more typical behaviours, he reacted to his father's moderate wine drinking by avoiding all alcohol, something he has maintained (with the exception of a few months at university) until today.

The teenage years

Jim's teenage years were not happy; he was unpopular. 'I was really cantankerous,' he admitted. He disliked being physically close to others, and he didn't know the names of most in his class, a result of the combination of a lack of interest and a struggle to remember names and faces that plagues him to this day. He did have a few friends in high school, 'to some extent. Very few. I had three friends I used to play bridge with in my last couple of years of school'. He was keen on girls but 'hopeless' at interacting with them. He was awkward and clueless, and being at an all-boys school didn't help. 'My greatest wish was to know what girls were thinking. I just had no idea,' he said. He would have crushes for months and even years, without ever asking them out. 'They probably didn't even know...' Jim added.

There were two positive influences in these years. The first was reading, often a book a day. 'It was before the age of computers; we didn't even have a television until my late teens. I was a fanatical reader,' Jim said. Jim read books about history, particularly ancient history, and was also interested in biology.

Then there were the great writers such as Tolstoy, Hemingway, Murasaki Shikibu (author of *The Tale of Genji*, an eleventh-century Japanese classic) and others.

The books Jim read sparked him to ask some unusual questions for a teen, such as,

Why does a civilisation collapse? Why did ancient Athens and the Roman Empire decay? Why do humans react to wealth differently to how animals react? When you put animals in an environment with masses of food, their populations explode. Humans are the only species where, when in an abundant environment, our populations, overall, shrink. So I just used to read masses and masses of books. A lot of science fiction too, of course; it wasn't all instructive.

The second positive in his teenage years was his relationship with his mother. He would come home from school and talk to her in the kitchen, pacing up and down or sitting at the kitchen bench. 'She was the person I was closest to in those times,' Jim said.

Jim was very idealistic and ferociously egalitarian in his thinking. He dreamed of a truly egalitarian society where university professors would take out the rubbish and cleaners take their turns at management. 'I dislike inequality,' Jim said.

In one interview Jim claimed he had no financial ambition when he was younger, certainly no notion of ever going into business. 'I never thought of becoming wealthy,' Jim said. But he did expect to be successful. He remembers listening to successful people on speech day and thinking, "That will be me one day". I just didn't expect success to come out of a lawn-mowing business!' Jim exclaimed.

Jim and SUCCESS

For Jim, the key to success is clear:

People think the key to success is knowing things, and that does matter, but the real key is temperament. If someone has the right character they can learn what they need to know. If they don't, no education will help...

My best staff are not those who have the highest degrees or the most experience. They're the ones with the best character. We waste billions on education trying to train up people's knowledge as if knowledge is what counts, and yet we undermine character by not letting kids get jobs, for example, where they would learn character...

One of the key goals of my research is to give people the tools to develop their character and thus level the playing field. Change character, and you can change the world.

Jim believes his own success is largely due to an unreasonable passion for customer service.

When I was mowing lawns I wanted to do a *great* job, I wanted to make it look terrific. I find that in business the people who succeed the best are not those who are most money hungry, but those who are actually dedicated to doing things well. It's not just that they don't want to let the customer down, they want to do a fantastic job for their own pride and self-respect.

As a teenager Jim wanted to be a science fiction writer. When he saw a typewriter on the dining-room table he asked his older sister, Lynne, 'How do I use this thing?' She showed him where to put his fingers, and within half an hour he was touch-typing. His passion for writing drove him to excel in English for his last two years of school, though he said that he didn't apply himself much otherwise. 'I struggled with laziness and would rather read science fiction than study. I got okay marks, but nothing like as good as if I had put my mind to it.' He was, however, in the elite class at Melbourne Grammar — something he didn't tell me, but his classmates did.

More than anything Jim felt a profound sense of alienation at school. He remembers sitting at an event, overlooking the dance floor on a rare date with his second cousin and thinking, 'These people are not my people, and their Gods not my Gods', which is a misquote from the Book of Ruth in the Old Testament.

He really liked his second cousin, 'but after that her mother kept us apart, obviously because we were too closely related, though I didn't realise it at the time. As usual, I was totally clueless,' Jim said.

Jim's second son, Andrew, said,

You get a sense of how separate Dad was, even from a relatively young age. He has occasionally expressed to me with what might be sadness, or regret, about his inability to relate to the people around him.

As a teen, when family friends visited, Jim took their kids to the park, greatly impressing their parents, 'but in reality I simply found children easier to get on with than adults,' Jim said.

Jim was seventeen and in his last year of high school when he watched the moon landing, which should have been exhilarating for a science-fiction-loving teen. But his reaction was different:

> People were thrilled we had pulled off this amazing feat, and that we would go on and on into space and the galaxy. But I remember thinking, 'This isn't going to last, there's something really wrong'. I didn't exactly know what, it was a vague feeling in those days ... Something about the decline of Rome and the parallels I saw from my reading.

2

The Accidental Gardener

Jim graduated from high school with utter jubilation. 'My last day of school was a wonderful feeling. I never had to go back!' He'd realised he lacked the discipline to be a science-fiction writer so had to figure out what to do instead. The question of why Rome had fallen and how civilisations form, grow, prosper and ultimately collapse, had been a constant passion since the age of fourteen. He resolved to go to university to study whatever would answer his questions ... But first he wanted a gap year. His parents had friends who owned a farm in Western Australia and he decided to work there for a time. It was there he began going by 'Jim' because the farmer's son was also called David. 'I wanted to create a new identity for myself,' Jim shared, signifying his desire to break away from childhood.

The work on the farm was great; Jim enjoyed being outdoors and doing physical work. He learned to drive, and found a horse in one of the paddocks he could ride. That far from the city the stars looked brilliant, and he learned the names of the bright stars and constellations from a book his father had given him. But even for

Jim it was too isolated, and after four months he returned home to Melbourne, not sure what to do next.

He saw an ad in the newspaper for a commission-only job selling encyclopaedias, and 'knocked on doors for two weeks without any success'. He didn't earn any money from it, so he started canvassing for a paint company, and failed at that also. 'I had no people skills, I couldn't take rejection and I absolutely hated selling. I was a thoroughly awful salesman,' Jim said. So he turned to what he knew: gardening. The last time he had done gardening jobs was in Adelaide five years earlier. What to charge? He had made $18 a week plus keep on the farm, so he figured charging $1.50 an hour for gardening work was reasonable, considering he would be using his clients' lawnmowers. 'I hand-wrote a notice with my price and the services I could do, and asked the man at the local hardware store to put it in his window,' Jim said. This marketing effort generated three clients, which was not enough to earn any kind of good wage. Two of the three became regular clients, and he hunted for other work to do for the remaining six months before university.

Jim got a job in the public service, which included three tasks: to help organise overseas travel, to help the man who did departmental publications and to make sure there were no long-distance phone calls on managers' phone bills. The tasks only took him half the week to complete, and there was nothing else to do. 'The public service was incredibly slack. We were told when an inspector was coming and we had to look busy,' Jim recalled with disgust. After a few months they promoted the man in charge of publications, which meant he merited a full-time assistant, which was to be Jim, but he refused. 'I said, "You've got to be kidding, being his assistant would only take a day a week!" I couldn't stand to have so little on.' They relented and Jim stayed in his existing role.

Later Jim discovered that the guy who had this role before him had organised it so that the only task he had to do was check the phone bills — which took fifteen minutes a week. 'He did it for a couple of years, and then just quit. That made me realise how badly the public service worked. It was horrifying,' Jim said. But it gave Jim an important lesson he would remember later on: the larger the enterprise, the more inefficient it tends to become. And this is especially the case when the person in charge has nothing to gain from efficiency.

University days

In 1971 Jim began studying sociology at La Trobe University. He lived at college for a few years, then shared student housing, supporting himself. He had refused financial support from his father. Throughout his undergrad Jim continued to mow lawns for the two clients he had gained on his gap year, even raising his hourly rate from $1.50 to $2 an hour. 'One of my clients objected, but I managed to blame it on inflation,' Jim said. Through word of mouth he gained more clients.

His high school results had meant he could have gone to the esteemed Melbourne or Monash universities, which all his peers did. A few of his classmates told me that Jim had gone to Melbourne University, and were surprised when informed it was actually La Trobe. Even at this age social pressures and norms had no effect on Jim. He chose La Trobe because it specialised in sociology and he wanted to learn how and why societies work, rise and fall. Despite all the books he had read, none of their explanations made sense.

But he came to realise that sociology didn't make sense either. 'It was and is complete rubbish. There's nothing empirical about it. It's just ideas, with no relationship to the real world. There's no testing, no empiricism!' Jim told me passionately. He remembered an assignment he had to do on Marxism, and he went to his lecturer in frustration, saying, 'The theory doesn't fit the historical evidence!' The lecturer replied, 'Marxism is not empirical, it's dialectic. It doesn't have to fit the facts'. To Jim this was idiotic. Why study something that doesn't relate to the facts? Jim wanted to figure out why Rome had fallen, and the best way to do that, he decided, was to study history extensively and look for the patterns himself. He switched his major from sociology to history.

Jim's first few months at university were the most social of his life. Coming from all-boys schools, he was suddenly in a world full of girls! 'I got very social and came to know lots of different people,' Jim said. He was on 'visiting terms' with dozens of girls in Menzies College, where he was staying. He went to parties for the first time and even drank alcohol, though he never got drunk. 'I never liked the taste of alcohol, and certainly not the effect,' Jim said.

His break into the social scene wasn't smooth. He had no understanding of what was considered normal behaviour or appropriate conversation. 'I remember asking a girl if she was pregnant, which was not very tactful. That's typical of me, just blurt out what was on my mind...' (She wasn't.)

Jim and some friends often played a board game called Diplomacy. The point of the game is to make alliances, and, if and when it suits you, to stab your allies in the back to profit from it. 'I would get ballistic and yell at somebody for stabbing me,' Jim remembered with deep embarrassment. He often cringes when looking back.

A lot of the stuff I did and said was really bad. Even little things that everybody takes for granted, like when you greet somebody and you say, 'How are you?' It's not really a question, but I didn't do that kind of stuff. I only do it now because I've learned it by rote, but it's never natural.

Jim even went through a phase of sporting an afro and walking around campus barefoot. 'He has always been extremely eccentric,' his daughter Sarah Penman said. 'I think he was just a bit of a hippie at university.'

Jim became friends with a girl at university who was the daughter of a dairy farmer, and fell for her deeply. Going to a dance with a group of friends, he watched her pair up with a guy who had clearly become her boyfriend. The agony of this led to weeks of despair, and he 'came out changed', he said.

He decided life had to have purpose, and social life was not giving him that. He became more solitary and started writing essays on 'Social Energy', his early concept of how society works. It was the start of a systematic attempt to understand social behaviour and social change, which was to become a lifelong mission. 'Those ideas are completely invalid now, but it was the origin of everything I've done since,' Jim said.

At the end of his first year at university Jim was finally able to win someone over, a sweet-natured girl 'who sang madrigals and had beautiful strawberry-blonde hair. She was wonderful. Very loving,' Jim remembered wistfully. They dated for eighteen months and were close, passionate and happy, but she was twenty-one and ready for marriage while Jim, at twenty, was not. He broke up with her 'in a brutal, uncaring way', he remembered with sadness and regret. It took him years to recover. For a long time he suffered bouts of depression with a constant sense of loneliness. 'I found the perfect girl but was too young to marry her. I never found anybody I liked as much, until I met my first wife ten years later,' Jim said. He still sometimes wakes up in the middle of the night with a terrible feeling of grief about how it ended. 'I feel so bad. She was wonderful. Really. She deserved someone far better than me.'

And according to Jim, that is exactly what she found. 'A few months after our breakup she married a great guy, my best friend at the time,' Jim said. He didn't mention a word of feeling betrayed by his friend, only sadness that he hadn't treated her right. 'If I'd have married her I never would have gotten divorced. Absolutely not. She's got the same qualities Li [Jim's current wife] has, in a way. She was a very giving sort of person. A principled, good, kind person. Just totally good.'

After their breakup he poured himself into his study. He refined and developed the primitive ideas of his first-year essay by looking at a wide range of societies, from China and Japan to Africa and Pre-Columbian America. His approach of looking at comparative patterns with a strong emphasis on demography was entirely at odds with the way history at La Trobe was taught.

In 1973 Jim began his third and final year of his undergraduate degree. The first thing he did was tell his lecturers, 'I'm not interested in coming to your courses. I just want to do essays on the subject matter on my own'. Amazingly, they accepted this arrangement, simply marking his essays. He loved the freedom to read up on history to the breadth and depth he desired, and everything he learned made it clearer to him that the modern West was parallelling the Rome of the late Republic.

Jim spent all his time reading and researching, an anomaly among his peers. With his now short hair and austere habits, he was at one time widely rumoured to be a 'narc', a narcotics agent. A girl at university once confronted him: 'Jim, you don't take drugs, you don't drink, you don't sleep around. Why don't you want to enjoy life?' Jim was dumbfounded by the question, telling me in our interview,

'To me, life must have purpose and meaning or it's not worth living. I just couldn't see the point of how she lived'.

By the time Jim completed his Honours thesis (for which he once again had to attend lectures and follow coursework), his ideas were complex and his thesis went far beyond the word limit, which did not impress the examiner. His ideas had crystallised around a single key concept: the nature of a society is not determined by its leaders, political and economic forces, or philosophies and ideas, but are driven by changes in the character of its people.

Jim and HIS PHILOSOPHY ON LIFE

Behind everything Jim does is a sense of duty. 'There should be a purpose to life, not just living to enjoy it,' Jim said.

I love my life: a wonderful wife, great kids, fascinating job. But happiness is not the point of life. People often think it is, but it's a miserable purpose. In fact, one study found that seeing happiness as life's purpose is especially common in alcoholics. That thinking leads to 'if I want a drink I'll have a drink', but it doesn't make you happy because short-term indulgence brings long-term misery. Whereas if you forget about happiness and live life with purpose, happiness becomes a by-product.

He then talked about the aspects of life most linked to happiness.[1]

People often think money is the key. It's not. Some of the most miserable people in the world are very, very rich. The third most important thing is community, the second a sense of purpose, and the first is relationships: with friends, family, spouse, and for me, God. Money doesn't even come in the top three! When you do things because they're the *right thing to do,* happiness comes.

The cutting edge

Honours year was crucial in another way. He had heard of people charging much more than his $2 an hour for mowing lawns, and decided to try to find more clients for the 'incredible sum' of $3 an hour. 'I used the duplicator at the university union to print small flyers advertising my services,' Jim recalled. He walked his parents' neighbourhood, dropping leaflets into letterboxes. 'The response was astounding! Many people said they had never heard of anyone working so cheap,' Jim remembered.

Jim still didn't own a car so he cycled to his clients and used their lawnmowers, as well as cycling to university. But it was time consuming. He was also frustrated he was getting nowhere with girls. 'I couldn't find anybody I liked,' Jim said. Perhaps a car could solve his problems? He persuaded his bank manager to lend him $1600 for a second-hand Holden Kingswood.

'The car didn't help at all with girls,' Jim admitted, but the need to pay for it brought a positive change to his business. He realised that if he moved from hourly rates to a fixed price per lawn he would be able to make more money — he could even charge $5 a lawn! Most lawns only took thirty minutes to mow, so it would earn him 'the dizzying' sum of $10 an hour. But to command such a price he would need his own mower, which would cost $200. It felt like a large sum when he already owed so much on his car, but it was necessary, so Jim bought a bright-orange lawn mower. 'It was the scariest decision of my whole business career,' Jim reflected with utter sincerity.

He printed and dropped leaflets that read 'Most lawns $5'. The response was good, and by working one to two days a week he paid off the mower and the car in six months. Exercise in the open air, which he enjoyed, also made a good break from studying.

Still, it had taken him four years to move from a low hourly rate to buying his own mower — not a great indicator of entrepreneurial brilliance. But he did have one habit that made a big difference: he cared deeply about doing a great job. He always mowed the lines straight, and picked up all the cut grass even if it was raining. He constantly looked for ways to give the lawns a cleaner finish, and was always punctual, showing up exactly when he said he would. 'Customers hate being let down, especially when they're waiting at home for someone who doesn't turn up,' Jim said. In twenty years of mowing for thousands of different customers, it only happened twice that he didn't show up — 'And I am sure it was only twice, because I can still remember the sense of horror I felt,' he said.

His biggest frustration was that he couldn't cut the edges nicely. It was 1974 and the only gardening tool for the job was an edging wheel. This did a decent job on mower strips, but not around trees and flowerbeds nor against retainer walls. 'It frustrated me greatly, but there was nothing I could do save spending half an hour with a pair of shears,' Jim said. None of his clients expected neat edges, but it bugged him. 'I remember standing there looking at a mowed lawn and thinking, "This isn't right". The finished look didn't satisfy me,' Jim said.

By the end of his Honours Jim had enough clients to sell some off in a batch to another independent as a 'mowing round'. The sale made him several thousand dollars, which together with an inheritance from his English grandmother let him buy a small weatherboard house in Eltham, 20 kilometres north-east of Melbourne. Jim loved the rustic lifestyle and later, according to his son Andrew, 'he would go into his backyard and make a fire, and cook his lunch on it. Even when it was raining he would go out with a beanbag over his head'. I asked

Jim if this was true, as a beanbag sounded improbable. 'A waterproof beanbag actually works quite well as an umbrella,' Jim replied sincerely.

A PhD in History

After completing Honours at twenty-two Jim decided to undertake a PhD, because he wanted a career in academia that would allow him to continue his research. His PhD topic was far from normal. A standard history thesis looks into a specific place and time in great detail, using original source material to expand understanding. But Jim wanted to research history as a whole to look for patterns that might explain the rise and fall of civilisations. 'I wasn't interested in reading masses about one specific time,' Jim said.

June Phillipp, the woman who had managed his Honours year, advised he was better off staying at La Trobe for his PhD, where they would more likely tolerate his strange approach. She also offered to act as his thesis supervisor. Jim said,

> This was very nice of her because she didn't have a clue what my theory was about, and never really came to grasp it. She was a lovely lady. I was prickly and difficult and impatient of social niceties — in fact I was hardly even aware of them. And still she volunteered to supervise me.

Jim is 'very lazy', he said often, and he struggled greatly with the discipline required for his PhD. His target was to research for at least thirty hours each week, which he found hard due to the concentration his research material required.

'Business is easy in comparison with research,' Jim said. 'In business you just sit there and do emails, take phone calls, talk to people and stuff. It's a breeze.' His fellow PhD students were deeply fascinated by their studies and worked day and night, but Jim struggled.

I'm lazy, I really am. I had this sense of duty, of responsibility. I thought these ideas were important and I should do something about them. They were interesting but really, really difficult.

He managed to meet his weekly target, though he didn't always stay on track. After reading history for hours and hours he would get bored and hunt for something else that was kind of on topic so he could have the excuse to read it in his study hours. That's how he began reading cross-cultural anthropology, 'which at the time I thought was just self-indulgent laziness,' Jim said. But he noticed the same patterns there that he'd seen in his history research. It was an exciting discovery and he read and read and read, until after a while that too became boring. The pattern repeated again with psychology, then zoology — 'and I started seeing connections there too!' Jim said exuberantly. 'Out of pure dogged laziness I managed to see connections among widely separated fields that people normally wouldn't see.'

Jim has an incredible memory for history. In one of our interviews he shared many examples, including dates, names, places, details, all off the top of his head. He rattled the examples off in quick succession, animatedly launching into the next example before I had finished digesting the last.

His studies made him realise that a society's ability to ward off invaders isn't purely to do with formal organisation, the size of the state or the physical technology. For example, why did the Spanish easily conquer the highly organised Inca in the sixteenth century, yet struggle with the scattered and relatively resource-poor Araucanians (in what is now Chile) for centuries? Why did the Spanish fail in their attempted conquest of the Netherlands, and why did Spain fight off the French at the start of the nineteenth century so fiercely? 'There was something in the psychology and attitudes of the people, in the way they supported their government or leader,' Jim said. He concluded it was the character of the people,

> a habit of mind where the individual is loyal to their culture and society, and not just to authority in general. This makes the state far more robust, and harder to conquer.

Yet character was always changing. Rome fell, in his view, because the character of the Romans in the fifth century AD was very different from that of the Romans in the Republic. But why?

To see what the evidence was, and make his own theories of *why* things had happened, he studied broad overviews of as many different periods in history as he could. But he found a lot of the existing historical research wanting. 'For example, historians describe the progress of thought from closed to open thinking, as happened in Europe over the past one thousand years.' But Jim couldn't ignore the counter-examples:

> The Sumerians, who lived in what is now Iraq in the third millennium BC, were brilliantly creative. They invented writing, the potter's wheel, the system of minutes and hours we still use today, and much more. China and India in the fifth to third centuries BC were hotbeds of new thinking in philosophy and religion, as well as technology. Later societies in these areas, with infinitely more people and wealth, were far more conservative. Why?

Jim saw a pattern in sexual behaviour. 'There is a correlation between sexual restriction and civilisation,' he said, 'and yet, when a society starts to loosen their sexual morality, they have this extraordinary flowering of culture'. Citing the examples of the late Roman Republic and Greece from the late fifth century to the fourth century BC, he found 'the same pattern as you get in the modern world: there is an initial economic and cultural flowering while sexual behaviour loosens'.

But in the ancient world after that flowering period, civilisation started to decay. 'Most modern historians do not see changes in sexual behaviour as the reason, though some Roman historians at the time thought it was,' Jim said.

> It seems to be a two-stage process. First, people become less rigid in their way of thinking but maintain their work ethic, so culture and the economy flourishes. Then, over succeeding generations, the work ethic declines along with the birth rate, and the civilisation declines.

What he couldn't understand was the *reason* for the delay. If sexual behaviour affected character, why did changes in sexual behaviour not have their full impact for several generations? This was the mid 1970s, 'decades before science was to come up with a way to make sense of this puzzle,' Jim said.

Jim's research also affected him in a more personal way. For nearly a decade he had been a militant agnostic, while strangely drawn to the idea of God. Now he began to suspect that Christian teachings in regard to sex and other areas, rather than being irrelevant and outdated, might have been one of the keys to the development of Western character, and thus civilisation. 'It was a deeply unsettling thought,' Jim said.

3

Jim's Calling

In 1977 Jim turned twenty-five. He was living in Eltham, in the third year of his PhD, and he felt ready to marry — only he couldn't find anybody he liked. It was deeply frustrating. 'I was getting absolutely nowhere, and the years were passing,' Jim said. He regretted the choice he'd made at twenty to break up with his then girlfriend. Why couldn't they have met when he was ready for marriage? 'I missed her badly. I couldn't believe how difficult it was to find anybody I liked,' Jim said.

His introversion didn't help. He hated parties and didn't have the courage to approach girls. Plus, his research was his main focus. 'I didn't have much of a connection with the wider world,' he said. His goal was to finish his PhD and begin his academic career, hopefully finding the right girl along the way and having children. (He couldn't wait to be a father — in fact, later, when he was newly married, he became a sperm donor as 'a public service', as he said).

He was mowing lawns one day a week, enough to fund his frugal lifestyle. This frugality has stuck: even today he hates spending money, buying home brand at the supermarket despite his family's preference for better-quality products. 'In those days I never spent *anything*,' Jim said. This did not, however, extend to his fledgling business. He didn't look after his mowers well and they often needed repair. He always went to the same mower shop in Eltham, owned by a bloke called Tom. 'You know,' Tom told him once, 'you look after your customers better, and your mowers worse, than any contractor I know.'

Another time, while waiting for his mower to be fixed Jim saw a 'weird looking piece of equipment' in the corner of Tom's shop. It had a long pole, a handle in the middle, a little engine on one end, and on the other was a plastic contraption with a cord sticking out. 'What's that?' Jim asked.

'A brushcutter,' Tom replied.

'A what?'

'One of the first in the country. I just got it in from Japan.' Tom showed Jim how to hold it, explaining, 'The white nylon cord at the bottom swings around really fast and cuts the edges without hurting the trees'.

Jim nearly jumped with excitement. This contraption would mean he could finally cut the edges around trees, clotheslines and retaining walls! It cost much more than Jim expected, but he bought it on the spot and was one of the first people in Australia to own a 'whipper snipper', as it soon came to be known. 'I could cut *all* the edges, a job the customer themselves could not do!' Jim exclaimed. He not only cut the edges, he snipped grass from cracks in driveways and blew the cut grass off, leaving the property spotless. 'I remember customers saying, "I never knew my lawn could look this good!"' Jim told the crowd at a Jim's Training, where he shares the story. 'Finally, I could produce a look I was totally satisfied with.'

But lawn mowing was still a side interest: a way of earning money and getting exercise. Research remained Jim's number one focus, and he was finding more and more evidence that character is the key to history.

Jim saw that periods of chaos in a society followed a pattern: a slow decline into feudal disorder followed by a swift rise to national unity. 'China, in particular, showed it in the rise and fall of the major Tang, Sung, Ming and Qing dynasties,' Jim said. England showed the same pattern several times over, such as the decline of central authority in the late fourteenth and fifteenth centuries followed by swift recovery after 1485.

What Jim found most fascinating of all, where evidence existed, 'was the connection between this political pattern and a demographic one,' Jim said. Periods of high birthrate and low deathrate, for example England in the early thirteenth century, and the sixteenth and nineteenth centuries, alternated with periods of low birthrate and high deathrate. In every case he could find, he saw the peak of feudal disorder came 'ninety years before the midpoint of the growth period'. There were other patterns as well. 'Major wars tended to break out around twenty years after the year of maximum growth,' Jim said. Russia and Germany both reached a peak level of population growth in the 1890s. In 1914, the Great War broke out. Japan reached a similar peak in 1926, attacking Pearl Harbor just fifteen years later.

This was when Jim's dalliance in zoology became pertinent. He was reading about regular population cycles in small animals such as lemmings and muskrats, 'And you know what?!', he exclaimed exuberantly, 'They have the same pattern!' Periods of high birthrate and low deathrate alternated with the reverse, 'and there was even the same boldness just after peak growth!'

This was a major breakthrough. 'There was the same pattern in China, the same pattern in Europe and the same pattern in muskrats!' Nobody else seemed to think there was any connection, but Jim was gripped by the possibility of there being '*one* reason to explain them all!' For his PhD thesis Jim called these 'dynastic cycles', though years later he renamed them 'lemming cycles'.

Jim was starting to believe that a great mass of historical evidence could be explained by an underlying biological pattern. 'This also meant that the theory could be tested!' Jim said. The idea that pheromones could possibly explain why local populations cycled together was later confirmed by experiments, with fascinating implications for the treatment of mental illness.

Coming to God

While these ideas were developing, a profound personal change took place. Though Jim was agnostic, his studies had made him accept many Christian values. But in 1979 he had a transformational experience and became a committed Christian, joining the Christian Union committee at La Trobe. His spiritual hunger was finally filled. He described this as a joyful, exhilarating time of his life when he enjoyed close friendships and gained a profound sense of purpose.

However, becoming Christian didn't improve his social skills, which, Jim will freely admit, are poor to this day. 'I can still be obnoxious, without meaning to, and people get upset at me sometimes,' Jim said. He doesn't have a sense for social tact. 'I don't know what appeals to other people. I became a Christian, but that didn't make me a particularly pleasant person.'

In the Christian community he was finally able to meet girls with traditional values. They didn't drink much alcohol, and were principled. In his words, 'it was like going from the desert into the promised land'. According to son Andrew, 'He went to church and found a whole different type of person there and that's...where he met Mum'.

It was a year later that he met seventeen-year-old Felicity Lawson through his Baptist Church Youth Group (where he was actively involved). They began dating and were very close and affectionate, 'in a proper way', Jim made sure to add. 'We didn't do anything we shouldn't have.' Felicity was also a very strong Christian, which was the core of their relationship. Jim recalled that Felicity was fascinating to talk to. 'She's very intelligent, she's got an incredible IQ.'

A ruined career

Jim's PhD was in History, but the implications of his theory were to do with Biology. With such a broad field of interest, Jim 'had no potential for an academic career'. He was twenty-nine and in love, but his career was in tatters. Over the preceding decade he had worked towards a career in academia so he could continue researching, publish his ideas and test his theories in a lab. But a conversation with a Sciences academic brought reality home: the kind of experiments Jim wanted to conduct would be so expensive it was unlikely an academic post would pay for them. If he retrained as a scientist he could conduct the research himself, making it far more affordable, but that would take another decade of study with no guarantee his project would ever be funded.

While other people might see the situation as a dead end, Jim saw a way through. Jim decided that he would, somehow, have to become rich. Rich enough that he could fund the multimillion-dollar research himself.

'Until that time I had absolutely no financial ambition,' Jim told me. 'It never even crossed my mind that it was worthwhile becoming wealthy. I didn't like spending money, I still don't buy stuff.' But he believed that his work was vital for the wellbeing of society, and he had to pursue it. Business was the obvious arena to make millions in, not his mowing business — which that wasn't going anywhere but perhaps another business.

Still, he finished the last work on his thesis and submitted it, while continuing to mow lawns part time, only for it to be rejected.

The people who marked it had no idea what to make of it. Usually the comments on a dissertation are several pages long, but two of the three markers only wrote a paragraph. The third wrote more but didn't like Jim's methodology, adding that if Jim's thesis had been 'a magnum opus at the end of a distinguished career', Jim remembered, 'it might have been acceptable, but for this unknown person to challenge every idea that historians had lived by?'

I asked Jim if it was incredibly crushing, after eight years of work, to have his thesis rejected. 'No,' was his short reply, before reiterating that it simply meant he would have to become very rich himself. I wonder if the passing of thirty-six years has mellowed his memory of what it was like at the time, or if he genuinely was not upset when his thesis was rejected. I know I would have been heartbroken, but Jim has a very different temperament.

Jim and WEALTH

Jim believes wealth undermines character.

> Wealth is corrupting, leading to leisure and luxury and undermining character. It also builds pride, making people think they're better than others. And it's especially corrupting of children, which is why we try very hard to live a normal life. My kids know at some theoretical level that we're rich, but it's nothing like the lives of the rich and famous they see on television! And they never tell people who their father is, unless they're specifically asked.

Esther, his fourteen-year-old daughter, said the same:

> I don't like people knowing who Dad is, and Dad doesn't either. I've only told three people, and that's only because I didn't want them to find out and be freaked out.

Sylvia, his sixteen-year-old daughter, told me a story about how low-key he is:

> One time at the airport he was wearing his uniform, and the security guy scans him and says 'Oh, you work at Jim's?' and Dad said 'Yeah', and the guy kept probing, 'Oh wow, what's it like working there? Is there actually a real Jim?', and Dad just nodded and laughed and walked away.

The beard appears

With his academic career no longer an option, Jim turned to mowing lawns full time. By now he was back home living with his parents, having sold his house in Eltham to buy a block of land in Noojee, 100 kilometres east of Melbourne because he'd always wanted a place in the country. He put an old, re-established house on the block and advertised his gardening services with leaflet drops in his parents' neighbourhood and ads in local newspapers. Clients poured in the door, and he got so busy he decided to bring on contractors who used their own equipment and paid him a 20 per cent fee. After years of rigorous, self-disciplined study, he was now free to indulge in some laziness. He was in love with Felicity, which was a total distraction, and decided he didn't even need to mow lawns. Instead, he 'stayed home to manage' his business.

Except he was terrible at it. He even hired someone to do the administration so he could sit on his beanbag reading science fiction. It was around this time that out of laziness he quit shaving and grew a beard. Felicity liked it. 'The lack of exercise made me lethargic and lazy,' Jim said. He started losing money, and as the months wore on he was forced to borrow thousands of dollars to stay afloat.

He eventually realised he had a business that was costing him money rather than making him rich. He decided to clear the debt by selling his customer base, something he had done in his student days. Hopeless at sales, he employed a professional salesman to do the job — but the salesman, after closing the deal, disappeared with Jim's money. Jim sold his Noojee property to keep his business afloat, but it still wasn't enough. He found himself $30 000 in debt, the equivalent of over $100 000 today, with no clients. 'I had owned a house, and a few years later it was gone and I was in debt. I felt pretty stupid,' Jim admitted.

Despite his dire financial situation, in December 1982, after dating for over a year, Jim and Felicity got married. Jim was thirty and she was nineteen. They were married in the North Balwyn Baptist Church with Jim's brother, Chris, as his best man, and had the reception at Felicity's parents' house. Not only was this a happy event in a dark time, it also proved an essential turning point; the responsibilities of marriage kicked Jim into gear. 'It gave me a sense of having to look after my family. I had to do whatever was necessary to survive. Marriage was good for me,' Jim said.

Determined not to repeat the mistakes of laziness and mishandled finances, Jim went back to mowing lawns. It was the only job he knew. But he would do it properly, while hunting for a better business idea that could make him rich enough to pay off his debts and fund his research.

Now, he only had $24 and a rundown Holden Kingswood, trailer, mower and whipper snipper to launch his new mowing business. He famously spent $4 on Letraset transfers and $20 on printing yellow leaflets advertising his array of gardening services — mowing, collecting rubbish, slashing and weeding — along with his contact number. He and Felicity were renting a house in Balwyn, and a few weeks before Christmas 1982 they dropped the flyers into nearby letterboxes.

Work flooded in. Felicity answered the phone and booked jobs while Jim mowed the lawns. The week after Christmas his trusty mower and whipper snipper both gave up the ghost. He bought replacements with what little money they had, and after leaving the store realised he had been undercharged $100. It was a gift from God: $100 he desperately needed! But it didn't sit right, so, after some hesitation Jim returned to the store and paid the remaining $100. Later that day, unasked for and out of the blue, a client offered to print $100 worth of leaflets for Jim for free. Jim saw this as a powerful sign of God's providence, and that doing the right thing would always somehow be rewarded.

He mowed lawns from morning till dusk, Monday to Saturday. He enjoyed being outdoors getting exercise, which he realised was essential to overcome his laziness. Today he is fervent about the value of exercise, either running on a treadmill or doing gardening work for at least half an hour a day.

In January 1983 Jim turned over $500 to $600 a week, enough to cover his debt repayments and their meagre living expenses. Jim registered his business under the name 'Balwyn Gardening', after the suburb he and Felicity rented in. 'I intended to focus on just one suburb, which gives you an idea of my ambitions for it!' Jim said. Thanks to his extreme obsession with leaving every job looking as perfect as possible, referrals came in thick and fast. He tried employing people to do the excess work, but they never finished a job as well as Jim wanted and didn't earn enough to cover the costs. He experimented with bringing on subcontractors again, this time staying out in the field mowing lawns himself too, but their customer service was even worse than his employees' had been.

Towards the end of 1983 June Phillipp, Jim's supervisor for his PhD, reached out with a suggestion. 'Look, if you rewrite the methodology section of your thesis, I think you should be able to get it through,' Jim recalled her saying. To do that Jim needed time off, which he couldn't afford.

He decided to sell a batch of his clients as a mowing round to earn a few thousand dollars. This time he didn't hire a sales rep; he advertised in the local paper, took calls and within a few weeks managed to sell it. But by the time the sale was made, through word of mouth and ongoing advertising, he was fully booked again with mowing clients. Perhaps he could sell these off too? He advertised again in the paper, and again, by the time the new guy was ready to take over, Jim was fully booked with mowing work! He sold off a third round of clients, surprised at his financial success.

Over the next few months Jim worked on his thesis and resubmitted it, then returned to mowing lawns. Five months later, in April 1984, Jim had an outstanding month: 'My thesis was accepted, I paid off the last of my debt and I learned I was going to be a father!' Jim exclaimed. They had a baby boy they named Richard.

Jim's thesis did not receive much attention. 'It was very disappointing. To me these patterns are so blindingly obvious! My theory could be confirmed or refuted by testing; no other theory of society came close!' But it would be twenty-four turbulent years before Jim had enough money to put his theories to the test.

4

This Little, Short-term Mowing Business

Jim continued mowing lawns and selling mowing rounds. 'Balwyn Gardening' became too narrow for the suburbs he was now advertising in, so he experimented with ads in the local paper for 'Jim's Mowing', and the phones rang hot. To give the impression of being nearby he employed local women to answer the phones, and put on subcontractors to service the clients until he had enough customers to sell as a mowing round.

Still, Jim wasn't going to become a millionaire selling mowing rounds. He had to find something else. He and Felicity moved out of the red-brick house in Balwyn and rented a shop in Surrey Hills with an apartment above it, with the idea of selling computers and offering lessons in how to use them. The shop failed, partly because Jim knew almost nothing about computers, and a later attempt to start a mower shop at a different location also failed, for much the same reason. 'I tried to get something else going besides this little, short-term mowing business,' Jim said.

They didn't enjoy living above the shop, and with the computer shop failing there was no reason to stay. They moved into a small house in

Blackburn that was 'very primitive, with uneven floors. But it had a nice garden,' Jim remembered fondly.

A year later they bought their first house, in Wolseley Crescent, Blackburn. The small bungalow in the backyard served as an office, and Jim's Mowing continued to progress. While still mowing lawns himself, Jim hired people to answer phones, drop leaflets and handle administration. He later expanded the office into an attached flat in their backyard to include more desks. He was often in the office taking calls himself.

By this point Jim and Felicity had three sons: Richard, Andrew and David, all with less than two years between them, and a daughter on the way. Felicity 'was devoted to the children, utterly selfless and giving,' Jim said. (Felicity declined to be interviewed for this book.) Jim admitted he often has no clue what people around him are thinking or feeling. 'If they talk to me, as Li [his current wife] does, I'll listen and try to help. But otherwise I can't easily tell. Obviously,' he said, referring to the fact that he and Felicity ultimately divorced, 'she wasn't happy'.

The brand was working well, but there were two major problems. Alarmingly, half the calls Jim received were complaints of lateness. As Jim remembered with frustration, 'most of my subcontractors simply wouldn't make a habit of turning up on time, no matter how often I asked them'. The other problem was that Jim continued to be bad at sales.

Selling by not selling

The breakthrough came from an unexpected place. Shortly after moving into their new house, Jim and Felicity joined the Church of Jesus Christ of Latter Day Saints, the Mormons. Since getting married they had attended the Baptist Church where they had met, 'but it wasn't rigorous enough for me,' Jim said. He had been reading about the Mormon Church and he liked the discipline and commitment, and, with his relationship with Felicity feeling increasingly distant, he needed a new outlet. After chatting with some Mormon missionaries Jim decided to join. He admitted he 'pushed Felicity into joining too'.

Jim said he 'never really accepted a lot of [the Mormons'] core teachings; their theology is weird'. The Book of Mormon says the Americas were settled from Judaea around 600 BC, while Jim accepts the standard view that Native Americans originally came from Siberia at least 10 000 years earlier. But he looked past it: 'I just loved the structure, the organisation, the people,' Jim said. He took on various teaching roles, including at one time teaching the main adult Sunday School class. 'Fortunately,' he said, 'that year it was on the Old Testament!'

Today Jim's view of religion is practical, rather than theological. (In yet another idiosyncrasy, despite being an evolutionist he currently attends an ardently creationist church in Chirnside Park.) Eric Skattebo, a close friend of Jim's from his current church, doesn't understand Jim's lack of interest in theology.

He's written a massive book on civilisations rising and falling, yet his faith is like a child's faith. He says 'I'm not into theology, I just want to know the practical things; how do I live a good life?' Mormons are even stricter than strict; they have rules like no caffeine, no tobacco, no alcohol…and he still follows that to this day. But when I visit his house he still offers me tea.

Jim hasn't attended the Mormon Church for fifteen years, but it left a strong impression. 'In some ways I still miss it,' he said. Despite finding the benefits of Mormonism compelling ('You know Mormons are far more likely to be successful and live longer? They're healthier. They have great family values. They're economically successful.'), Jim said he

> can't overcome my concerns about the Book of Mormon, which was obviously made up by Joseph Smith. Today I go to a church where they openly believe the world was created 6500 years ago and that Noah's Ark was real, which it wasn't. But I like the Church. I don't challenge the orthodoxy; I don't think God really minds about the theology, quite frankly.

The Mormon church also taught him, indirectly, what he regards as 'the single greatest lesson of my career'. Through the church he met Peter Rancie, who ran a successful advertising agency. Jim visited Peter to ask his advice, and for half an hour Peter told Jim everything he knew about advertising and generating leads, ending with the advice that he didn't think Jim needed an advertising agency yet. Jim left utterly convinced that if he ever did need an agency, Peter's would be the one. But as he walked back to the car he couldn't immediately see why.

> Peter hadn't actually told me anything about his agency. I didn't know what they charged or anything. But he'd completely sold me on it. How? You have to remember that at this time I was still struggling with my inability to sell mowing rounds. And then I realised that he'd shown no other interest than in the success of my business, and by doing this he'd completely sold me on his. Could this possibly work for selling mowing rounds?

Jim tried it on his next lead. Rather than telling the person why it was a great idea to buy from him, he simply asked questions and gave advice. 'I even told people to buy another business if it was a better deal,' Jim said. He wrote a short booklet on how to buy or build a mowing business, which he gave away to leads. Amazingly, people started calling him back to buy from him — 'even those I had recommended should buy elsewhere!' Jim exclaimed.

It worked out far better than I expected. I only tried it because I was too introverted and socially awkward to give a proper sales pitch, and it proved to be the best sales pitch of all! Because it was a genuine attempt to help them make the best decision, for them. It was this, far more than the decision to franchise or any other action, that has been at the core of my business success. It's something we teach every new franchisor. I call it 'Selling by not Selling'.

That is also the title of one of his books. From then on, Jim's sales tactic has been transparency and honesty.

After making some sales, Jim thought the people who'd bought from him would sell his mowing rounds better than he could. He wrote their names and numbers on small white cards and pinned them to a board in his office. When speaking with the next prospect, he suggested they choose however many names off the pin board they wanted to call, confident everyone would speak highly of Jim's offering and do most of the selling for him. And that is exactly what happened.

Jim and SMALL TALK

Jim does not like shaking hands, being physically near anyone but family, or small talk. 'He told me he would rather have a root canal,' his friend Eric Skattebo said, laughing.

Jim's very friendly, but yet...sometimes he maybe doesn't know how to be, because relationships are not his strongest suit. It can be odd, but I know he's well intentioned.

(continued)

Jim and SMALL TALK *(cont'd)*

Cleaning franchisor Nicole Wood shared that

He's short and sharp, he's always busy and he just doesn't quite have the sensor to think, 'Oh yeah, maybe I should ask, how is she today?' He doesn't have the mechanism to do that.

However she went on to add, 'When you get chatting to him and he warms up to you, he is good fun'.

Sharon Connell, the divisional for Dog Wash, explained that 'he's not one to sit around and chat, but if you engage about business he has lots to say, and lots of good guidance'. But she also shared an awkward moment. At a franchisor's conference she was having a cup of tea on a break, and Jim was next to her.

I didn't know what to say, so we just stood next to each other in silence, until I went, 'Hi Jim' and he went 'Hi Sharon, things are going well'. I said, 'Things are going really good' ... and then we just stood there in silence!

Haydar Hussein, the divisional of Cleaning, recalled walking between buildings at National Office when Jim called out 'Haydar!' in greeting. Haydar walked over and Jim asked him a question, which he started to answer when Jim's wife walked by in the distance. Haydar said,

Jim saw her and walked to her. I was halfway through replying — he didn't even say goodbye. I was still talking as he walked away; it was like he deleted me from the whole scene. I thought that was weird.

Phil Maunder said that Jim is

single focused. In a lot of ways he's an incredibly boring person. You can't really talk to him about anything except business. We always knew he was strange ... It's just very hard for him to develop relationships.

Many interviewees explained that Jim is not good at personal conversations, he won't think to ask staff how their weekend or holiday was. This can lead to issues with staff, who struggle to connect with him. But despite Jim's lack of 'personality' and small talk, and his inability to easily make people like him, he in no way lives a lonely life. Jim has a happier marriage than most, and spends a lot of time with his children every week, either when he's working from home or driving them places. He has close friends through his church who all meet once a week at his house. He is always up for a game of chess with staff, and will on occasion invite a group of staff to a Saturday at his farm to play board games together.

Still, as Anthony Silverman, a franchisor, said, 'Jim will be active in the conversation, but as soon as somebody brings up football or the weather, virtually anything else, he'll walk off'. Jill Stallworthy, the manager of Jim's call centre, said,

If you say to him, 'I've been on a holiday,' he'd say 'oh' and that's it. But if you say, 'I've got an idea about customer service', he'll talk to you for half an hour. He's driven by it.

Over the years Jim has surprised many a staff member and franchisor with his wealth of knowledge in many different areas, and with his utter ignorance of sport. Craig Parke, who had many roles with Jim's over the years, recalled driving into Melbourne with Jim and 'Jim asked, "What's that building there?" and I said, "That's the MCG". I mean, fuck'.

A franchise is born

It was around this time that VIP expanded from Adelaide to Victoria and Jim decided to launch his own franchise system in self defence.

Armed with an understanding of how he could add value to franchisees that would make their monthly fees worthwhile, he employed a solicitor and started hammering out a franchise agreement.

In Jim's view most franchise agreements are geared towards the franchisor (the corporate office), leaving franchisees with few rights. Franchisors can change the terms of the business, provide no guarantee of income and severely limit franchisees' potential for growth. Also, franchisees have no right of renewal at the end of the term. Jim, motivated by his sense of right and wrong and hatred of inequality, felt that was unfair and asked himself, 'What would I want as a prospective franchisee?' He'd want clear territory rights, a guaranteed income, proper use of the advertising budget and to be protected from arbitrary contract changes. He'd also want the franchisor (corporate office) to not be able to raise franchisee fees beyond the rate of inflation, and he'd want to build his franchise as big as he desired, employing as many people as he wished, without having to pay any more in fees. 'It will be their effort that builds the business, not mine, so why should they pay more?' Jim explained to his surprised solicitor. Jim realised that the key to success was to attract and keep the best franchisees, because they would do a great job and build the reputation of the brand. Jim 'wanted to design a system so good you'd be mad not to join'.

Jim added a guarantee of franchise renewal at no cost, provided they were compliant, and absolute rights to their client base — meaning the franchisees, not Jim, had the rights to the clients and could walk away at any time with those clients. This was unheard of and considered business suicide. His solicitor asked, 'How will you stop people from building their business with you, and then going independent to avoid the ongoing fees?'

'I should have to earn the fees by the service I give my franchisees, which will only work if the fees are, in effect, voluntary,' Jim told his bewildered solicitor.

There was much arguing back and forth. His solicitor's job was to protect Jim's interest, and all Jim wanted to do was protect his franchisees. Jim had to fight for his radical clauses, and his solicitor kept arguing back, 'You're being too nice! You're giving them too many rights and too much power! You've got to water this down'. But Jim wanted something completely unlike any other franchise contract, and wouldn't be swayed.

After nine months of arguing, in June 1989 Jim finally had a franchise agreement he was happy with. It was at this time that Jim stopped mowing lawns himself, fifteen years after buying his first mower. But money was tight and launching a franchise wasn't easy.

Jim financed the franchise himself. In many ways he had already been franchising for the past five years: people who bought his mowing rounds received manuals, advice, training and help with resales. Now that he had the contract drawn up, all he needed was a logo, information brochure, uniform and trailer.

In the past, when experimenting with different styles for his newspaper ads and leaflets, he'd found the ones that included a photo of himself, complete with beard and hat, got the best response rate. So that was his starting point for the logo. A photo can't be put on a uniform, so he hired a photographer to take his photo and a graphic artist to turn it into a drawing. He stuck multiple options around the office, each using a different font, to find which was easiest to read. Thus, without much thought, a brand that would one day be recognised by millions was born.

To get an idea of what was expected on an information brochure Jim reviewed the VIP brochure he'd received at the 1988 franchising expo. He pulled it apart and rewrote it. For the uniform Jim simply added his logo to standard green work wear.

The trailer took more effort. He'd redesigned his own trailer over the years, constantly looking for improvements that made it easier to use. When mowing lawns he hadn't wanted his mower in the body of the trailer, taking up space that would be better used for garden waste, so he'd built a platform for the mower across his tow bar. 'But that made it hard to reverse so I got the tow bar extended,' Jim said. As time went by an edge was added to the platform, and then a cage, and then separate compartments for the whipper snipper and tools. 'Thirty years later we're still working on the design. Just recently we added galvanised floors and two-pack paint coatings to extend life,' Jim said. The functionality of his trailer design is so good that it has been adopted by many independents, something Jim is proud of.

Space for advertising wasn't considered when the trailer was designed, yet for close to thirty years you could argue that it was those trailers that built the Jim's brand. If National Office were to pay for the advertising it receives from its almost 4000 franchisees' trailers and cars, the estimated cost would be more than a million dollars a day.

To get franchisees, Jim approached his best subcontractors and operators who had bought mowing rounds from him in the past. At his first information evening sixteen people piled into the small back room of his home office, and Jim gave them an offer he hoped they couldn't refuse. Those who had bought a mowing round business in the past could swap it for a franchise, costing them nothing in start-up expenses but the signage for their trailers. If it didn't work out they were free to walk away and become independent again.

Jim handed out copies of his franchising agreement and asked for feedback. He had designed the best and fairest franchising agreement his solicitor had ever heard of, but still those present 'pulled it apart,' Jim recalled. 'They wanted more protection for their territory rights, for their rights to regular clients and against unfair termination. I was amazed by how much I hadn't thought to include'.

Jim went back to his solicitor to make those changes, and took the updated contract back to the sixteen who had been at the meeting. 'About half of them signed up,' Jim said. He had a franchise.

Jim put a small ad in the business opportunities section of the paper for a lawn mowing and gardening business, and enquiries came in. One of them was from Phil Maunder. It was 1989, and 'in those days it was a pretty unique business — there weren't many people doing it professionally,' Phil said.

Phil drove out to Jim's Blackburn address, finding a house on a suburban street. 'I remember rolling up and it was obviously the right place because it had a trailer in the front yard — but the garden was a complete mess,' Phil recalled. 'Inside, the office wasn't much better. Everything was old and the chairs were falling to bits... It was very backyard-ish.' Phil saw Jim had a couple of staff, and Jim invited Phil to his desk. 'He made room on his desk by simply pushing all his paperwork to the side,' Phil remembered.

It was very messy. But it was his enthusiasm that sold the business; when I left I knew I would buy a franchise. He wasn't trying to sell it; he was just incredibly enthusiastic and determined that his business was going to be successful, and he gave me the confidence that I could be successful in the business. From memory, I was franchisee number twelve or thirteen. It was very small back then.

Jim's ambition was modest. 'Jim said his aim was one hundred franchisees,' Phil recalled. 'At that stage it seemed like a long way away, but he was certain he would achieve it.'

Jim wanted to give his franchisees the best price for new mowers, so he made a deal with Ron Sadowski, the then owner of a Honda dealership in Melbourne called Kew Mowers.

Ron realised that this guy buying his mowers had something good going, and asked if Kew Mowers could do the servicing and repairs for Jim's franchisees in the area. Jim was happy with Ron, a salt-of-the-earth man with an easy laugh and a great Scottish accent, and recommended him, though 'they came voluntarily,' Ron assured me. As the months rolled on Ron got talking with 'the lads' about the work and how much they earned, 'and it was crazy money they were doing!' Ron exclaimed. 'All of a sudden I'm seeing Jim's everywhere!' He decided he wanted out of the shop and into Jim's Mowing.

I asked Ron what he thought of Jim back then. 'I thought he was brilliant. He was — the word's probably not "robotic", but A is A, B is B. Never a massive conversationalist.' Ron thought Jim's Mowing was worth expanding interstate, but Jim didn't want to. 'He was happy just doing Jim's in Victoria,' Ron said. 'We actually suggested early on that he should get other divisions, but Jim didn't want to do anything but mowing.'

Jim's research was always in the back of his mind, and he continued reading to develop his theories further, sometimes going to Monash University and reading about the social behaviour of monkeys and apes. It was five years since his PhD had been accepted, but he'd made no progress in finding a business that would make him rich. Jim set up a DIY research lab in his garage and began writing a book to further his ideas, which was published a few years later in 1992. 'It was pretty crude actually,' Jim said, 'I attempted to make a popular book but it didn't work'.

Jim's egalitarian thinking influenced the franchise. He held monthly meetings where franchisees could voice their opinions and concerns, and let decisions be made by vote. Today, Jim still takes great pride in his democratic process, though agreeing it's more of a 'consultative dictatorship'. Many decisions are still decided by vote, but ultimately Jim does what Jim decides is best for Jim's.

From his perspective,

> There are two kinds of decisions you make in franchising. One is core, which has to do with the integrity of the system, service to franchisees, service to customers, selection of franchisees, collecting of fees, anything you can't compromise on.

The second is everything else, which is non-core. For non-core decisions Jim gets input from as many people as possible to get a range of opinions. 'Franchisors and franchisees see things differently and come up with different objections,' Jim said.

> By listening to their concerns I get better decisions and people are on board. If someone says 'I don't like this', I'll say, 'Take it up with the advisory committee [an elected committee of franchisors] and have them vote on it'. Sometimes they say, 'Oh, but you

should make this decision yourself'. It's funny, they're all against democracy when they think I agree with them.

Ron Sadowski, who has been a franchisor in Jim's Mowing for twenty-eight years, said that in the advisory committee 'Jim obviously has the final say, but it isn't cut and dry. It's open to negotiation'. Jim is also proud of the fact that Jim's is the only franchise system in the world, to his knowledge, that lets franchisees and franchisors veto changes to their manuals. And that's only after the changes have first been approved by the advisory committee.

A flawed business model

The spring of 1990 saw work flooding in. The office system was basic: every few days, franchisees would call the office to put in for the kind of work they wanted to do in the coming days — for example, mow lawns in Epping, or mow lawns and remove trash in Richmond, Hawthorn and Kew. The office staff would then record this on a blackboard. When a customer called with a job, they wrote it on a slip of paper and put it in a margarine container. Then they would match the slips of paper with the jobs on the blackboard and, after assigning the job to a franchisee's code, the slip was moved to a lunch box. Finally, once the job was dictated to the franchisee, the slip was put into a billy can.

However it was easy to lose track of the loose slips of paper when things got busy, which happened frequently in the spring of 1990. If someone called to cancel a job, they had to hunt madly through the different containers to try to find the slip of paper with that job written on it.

Another systems issue was that many customers wanted same-day service, but in those pre–mobile phone days, Jim couldn't reach franchisees during the day when they were out on jobs. He couldn't expect his franchisees to call the office multiple times each day just in case another job had come in, so Jim proposed they all buy pagers, which they agreed was a good idea. 'We thought we were so high tech,' Craig Parke, an early franchisee who has had many different roles at Jim's over the years, laughed.

Still, Jim knew they needed a better system — perhaps a network of computers so staff could log into a terminal and enter jobs directly. Jim found a computer company whose owner was friendly and easygoing, which, Jim said, 'is important when working with someone as eruptive as myself'.

Jim was shown how a software program could make running the franchise much smoother, and was ecstatic. 'Most amazing of all, jobs could be paged directly to franchisees!' Jim said. And so the blackboard, margarine container, lunch box and billy can were retired, and Franchise Management System 1 (FMS 1) was born. Jim was ahead of his time; not many Australian small business owners invested heavily in software in 1990.

That spring, at the Franchising Expo in Melbourne, two years after getting asked to leave the VIP booth, Jim had his own. He now had sixty franchisees — many more than he'd expected after one year of operating. 'The reason for my growth was clear; my franchisees were making money and liked the system,' Jim said. He made the cheapest display possible for the Franchising Expo, and spent the three days at the booth himself to save hiring someone. Dressed in his green Jim's Mowing uniform, he stood out in a sea of exhibitors in business suits. A number of people bought a franchise.

Soon after, Jim hired a consultant to review his business' finances; he hadn't yet calculated whether he had a sound business model.

The consultant concluded the business was heading for collapse; Jim wasn't charging enough in fees to cover costs. This issue had gone undetected because of the influx of cash from each new franchise sale. Though Jim had over sixty franchisees, he would need one hundred and fifty simply to cover costs. 'But with one hundred and fifty franchisees our expenses would have been more! It wasn't sustainable,' Jim said.

Remarkably, 'instead of taking the action any competent business owner would', Jim admitted, he filed the report 'and forgot about it' until it became impossible to ignore at the end of 1990. The Australian economy went into recession in the September quarter of 1990, and lasted a year. Jim's own bank, the State Bank of Victoria, was near collapse and in 1990 was bought out by the Commonwealth Bank.[1]

Jim's Mowing was now tens of thousands over its overdraft limit and seemed like a dead end, so when a prospective buyer approached Jim he was keen to sell. What stopped him was the objections from his franchisees. 'I was taken aback. I genuinely cared about their welfare but because I'm not good at personal relations I hadn't thought they appreciated my efforts,' Jim said. He borrowed money from his father, renegotiated the overdraft, and took out a personal loan of $20 000 at another bank to get through.

Finally, he looked hard at his financials and worked out that his monthly fees were half of what they needed to be. Then he had to tell his franchisees...Jim organised a meeting and stumbled through an explanation of why he would have to double the fees or go under. The franchisees, understandably, weren't thrilled. Many asked to see the numbers themselves, but Jim had not prepared them.

Afterwards a franchisee took Jim aside and explained how to prepare a presentation properly, including the numbers. Together they drew up a detailed plan for the next meeting. According to the terms of the franchise agreement, Jim needed 60 per cent to vote 'yes' to higher fees, or the change wouldn't be possible and the business would fold. He delivered his presentation exactly as he had been advised, and held his breath for the vote: 63 per cent approved the change.

Expanding interstate

By June 1990 interstate expansion seemed more sensible, capitalising on all the work already done for the manual, contract and office system. There was only one barrier: Jim was scared of flying. 'When boarding a plane I couldn't help but imagine, in great detail, the inevitable crash,' Jim said. 'It wasn't so much the fear of dying than the knowledge that all hope for my research project would die with me.' (This changed many years later when his son Andrew became interested in his research, and clearly capable of carrying it forward if Jim were gone.)

Jim invited his best franchisees to his house in Blackburn and asked if any of them were keen to move interstate to build up Jim's Mowing there as state managers. This was the first time another layer of management was proposed in Jim's; previously, he had been the only manager for all the franchisees. But with operations moving to other states, Jim knew he couldn't manage it all. Phil Maunder was at the meeting and chose Adelaide; someone else chose Sydney, and another Queensland. Phil moved to Adelaide on the long weekend in October 1990, 'the first Jim's Mowing guy there,' Phil said.'

In October Jim travelled to Sydney, Brisbane and Adelaide to run seminars to drum up more business. He travelled by train, except for the Brisbane to Adelaide leg, for which he braved a flight. At his seminars Jim taught how to run a successful mowing business, ending with a brief outline of the Jim's franchise system. 'I know quite a few VIP guys attended, but because I charged twenty dollars they actually helped fund my trips,' Jim grinned.

Interstate expansion was exciting, but not very successful. The franchisee in Queensland stopped almost before he'd begun, and the one in Sydney soon after. 'Local support seemed a key ingredient for success,' Jim said. Roughly six weeks after Phil started in Adelaide Jim called him. 'This state manager setup isn't working, I'm going to run the states from Melbourne. Or you could become a state franchisor?' Jim offered, inventing the concept of a state franchisor on the spot. 'I'll sell you South Australia.'

The state franchisor would basically act as Jim acted in Victoria — selling franchises to franchisees, with a personal stake in their success. However, they would still need to answer to Jim as the ultimate decision-maker and quality control officer.

'What do you want for it?' Phil asked, thinking it over.

'Fifty thousand. How much money can you find?'

'I could probably get ten thousand together.'

Phil bought the South Australian rights for $10 000 upfront, and $1000 for each of the next forty franchise sales he made. 'Looking at it now it was a pretty good deal for me,' Phil said, 'but in those days Jim's was brand new'. Jim described selling South Australia 'almost for free', given how much it came to be worth over the following decade. Of course, if Jim's Mowing hadn't become successful the deal wouldn't have been good. It was a risk Phil Maunder took, banking on the brand and his ability to grow it massively, and it paid off, despite the fact that

VIP was an established competitor in South Australia. Jim's Mowing stood out because of its income guarantee, the fact franchisees could walk away, and that the fees were set (rather than being a percentage of revenue). The contract was signed in December 1990, making Phil Maunder the first Jim's Mowing state franchisor. He set to work, and quickly showed good results.

This system was replicated in Western Australia. The first franchisee to set up there didn't make much progress, but in late 1991 husband-and-wife team Peter and Michelle Ferry took on the state as franchisors and saw success.

Though things were going well in Adelaide, Phil Maunder had one challenge: finding a good supplier for the mowing equipment. The mowing retailers in Adelaide 'were difficult to get along with,' Phil said. They saw contractors as a threat to their business, rather than as an opportunity. Frustrated with Adelaide suppliers, Phil called Ron Sadowski from Kew Mowers in Melbourne and arranged a deal for his franchisees with Ron. Through this Ron 'got involved', according to Phil, with Jim's Mowing in South Australia. According to Ron, he became a part-owner of South Australia.

'Phil was a great franchisor, he supported franchisees well,' Jim reflected. At one stage, Adelaide had more franchisees per head than Melbourne. 'It was good seeing my system and ethos of putting franchisees first working without my personal involvement. It was also humbling. He was doing it better than me!' Jim said. Craig Parke, a franchisee at the time, remembered that Phil 'ran a very good region. His enormous growth changed our thinking in Melbourne'.

In 1991 one of Phil's franchisees took on the rights for Queensland, with Phil as a part owner. 'I used to spend one week in Brisbane every month,' Phil recalled. But there were issues and Phil's franchisee decided to leave. Ron Sadowski was keen, so Jim sold Ron the Queensland rights for $75 000 on a $25 000 deposit. Jim had, again, enormously underestimated the value of the state. 'A few years later the Gold Coast alone was sold for $90 000,' Jim recalled.

Phil Maunder was still a part-owner of Queensland, and he and Ron did a deal. 'Ron gave me the part that he kind of owned in South Australia, and I gave him my part of Queensland,' Phil explained. Ron said, 'I ended up with a contract for Queensland and Phil had Adelaide'.

Around this time Ron and his then business partner, Calvin Leaper, thought a 131 number would be good for Jim's. But Jim said no, preferring to stay with his 1800 number. So Ron and Calvin went to Telstra and bought 131 546 (131 JIM) for $2000 themselves. 'And then Jim said "Oh, I like that, we'll use that then,"' though he never paid me back,' Ron laughed.

Jim didn't know, until I mentioned it, that Ron was ever involved in South Australia and Phil in Queensland. He thought — until April 2018, some twenty-six years later — that Phil alone had South Australia, and Ron Queensland. Ron laughed that in those early days there were deals 'that National Office didn't see'.

Anthony Silverman, who joined as a franchisee in 1992, explained that 'in the early years we were all learning. National Office became a bigger thing over the years'.

The early days of interstate expansion were challenging. The 1990 to 1991 recession was hitting Australia — and particularly Victoria — hard. Not only was the financial climate bad, so was the weather; the grass wasn't growing. Jim wasn't selling enough new franchises because of the recession, and he had large financial responsibilities. A year earlier Jim had bought over 100 acres in Marysville, 100 kilometres north-east of Melbourne, to set up a tourist resort there to make his millions. He had poured most of his previous years' earnings into it, spending tens of thousands on permits. It was money he desperately needed now, but didn't have. 'I made the most stupid financial decisions,' Jim said. 'You wouldn't believe anybody had done so many dumb things as me.'

Jim's franchise agreement also had an 'absolute income guarantee', which meant if franchisees' earnings dropped below a certain amount, he would top them up. Without enough grass to cut, requests for the income guarantee flooded in, and Jim couldn't pay them. Thanks to his solicitor, the franchise agreement also had an 'Act of God' clause that stipulated that, in extreme conditions such as drought, the income guarantee could be waived. For the first time, Jim enacted the 'Act of God' clause in Brisbane and Melbourne. As he wrote in his book *Every Customer a Fan*,

> this was the blackest day of my business career. The Franchisees felt betrayed, and I could not blame them ... I was right in terms of the contract, but it felt wrong.

Months later Jim would take the 'Act of God' clause out of the contract altogether — 'it wasn't right having it there in the first place' he said, adding,

> Many people suffered, but without it the business would very likely have failed. The key is to have the financial reserves to get through the tough times. In those days we just didn't.

For those months when it was enacted, many suffered. However, if Jim hadn't enacted it, would Jim's Mowing exist today? We don't know.

5

Divorce

By December 1991 the crisis was over. Jim's Mowing had grown steadily for the second half of the year, and the company's financials had improved. But a new crisis loomed.

In March 1990 Felicity had given birth to a daughter, Sarah, their fourth child. In 1991 they had bought a house in Wonga Park, 30 kilometres north-east of Melbourne. It was on 2 acres, with a half-built mudbrick building in the backyard that was to become the office. In 1992 Felicity was pregnant with their fifth child, James — however that year irreconcilable differences led to divorce.

The Marysville acreage and Wonga Park house were sold, but they were deeply mortgaged so little was left. To help raise money for the settlement Jim sold off sections of his Victorian region to successful franchisees, so they could become franchisors (as Phil Maunder was in South Australia and Ron Sadowski in Queensland). They became responsible for looking after their franchisees and selling more franchises in their region. Selling these franchisor rights 'actually made my income smaller,' Jim said, but it gave him some much needed upfront cash. He even proposed selling the national rights to a group of franchisors, but at the time National Office made virtually nothing and was a headache to run, so they declined. This proved fortunate, because those rights are now the core of his business.

A unique parenting style

Jim only saw his children on access visits, which he found incredibly painful — he missed them terribly. 'It was the worst time of my life. The grief of missing them still affects me today,' Jim said. When the children visited, he made the most of every minute. Andrew and Sarah recalled fun weekends with their dad. 'In many respects he was a very positive father figure,' reflected Andrew. 'He really was a great dad,' Sarah said. Jim told an ongoing historical fictional story every time he picked up the kids, which continued for over ten years. Jim weaved his five kids as characters into the ongoing story, which began in Ancient Egypt and travelled through all of human history, and then into an imagined future in space. (Jim's science fiction reading was an influence.)

'The level of knowledge required to rattle off history in such detail was enormous,' Andrew said. 'And the stories had certain moral messages in it...what the character did always required tremendous effort — and we'd get knocked down, you couldn't become too powerful.' (A reflection of Jim's moral dislike for structural power, which is interesting, considering how much power he wields.)

Sarah revealed another side of Jim, one that was always intent on embarrassing his kids in public. 'He would do the most ridiculous dance,' she told me, demonstrating by swaying her body from side to side and clicking her fingers, 'and he would say, "ah, yeah, groovy!"

and I would be so embarrassed!' The mental image of Jim doing this dorky dance and saying 'groovy' is priceless.

Perhaps because they only saw Jim on access visits, it seems from our interviews that their memories of him are overwhelmingly positive. 'Access visits are some of my fondest memories. It was the weekend and that's when you had fun,' Sarah recalled.

Jim's parenting style was unusual. He gave his children incredible freedom and a lot of responsibility within a tight structure of rules. 'He had this "tick system",' Sarah explained. Jim sat the kids down at the end of the day and gave them a tick for helping with chores, behaving properly, doing the most original thing 'for example, making a clay sculpture', or asking an interesting question. 'I think a tick was worth, in real currency, about twenty cents,' Andrew recalled. They 'swore by and loved' the elaborate system. 'And we felt like we had a lot of freedom, we were encouraged to be creative — and rewarded through ticks,' Sarah said.

A student of neuroscience, Andrew explained the benefits of this approach:

the children who don't do well aren't the poorest — it's those who have nothing in their environment which connects reward to effort. The dopamine pathways in their brain aren't wired to defer present indulgence for future reward, which makes it very hard to work. The tick system was designed to help instigate that. I will probably have a similar system when I have my own family because it rewards effort and behaviour in a way that is very tangible.

Sarah explained that Jim approaches problems without any regard for what's normal and established, instead using his own intellect, reasoning and lateral thinking,

And he did that with parenting. 'What do children do? What do they need? A certain amount of regimen and moral guidance.' We were very well behaved, but we didn't feel like it was a dictatorship; we all knew our role and what we had to do.

They knew the boundaries, too. 'It was a very small democracy,' Sarah said:

we could veto someone's punishment if the insult was directed at us, if we chose to be gracious. We used to vote by age on where to go for dinner.

Andrew recalled dinner times 'crowded around a small wooden table' where chaos was allowed but breaking moral rules was not. 'Even mundane swear words such as "bloody" would incur a ferocious rebuke, and we were forced to eat anti-nail biting ointment as punishment,' Andrew recalled. He remembered a time Sarah dropped a paddle pop stick in the garden 'and Dad literally roared at her; littering was an abomination'. They were allowed to go to the shops in bare feet and play in the rain, and Jim encouraged exercise at every turn. 'There was discipline, but it was also sort of wild,' Andrew recalled. 'It was a lot of fun, but no doubt things would have been different if he'd been around during the week.'

On family holidays in the forest they would hike, dam rivers, 'or work on a hut we built over many years,' Sarah said.

Dad would have us quietly cooperating as an efficient work force to achieve our collective goal. Looking back, he was a natural leader in that we never felt we were doing anything other than what we wanted. Even if that was carting heavy stones for hours. We felt useful and part of something greater than ourselves. They were the best holidays a kid could hope for.

A central feature of their time with Jim was being outdoors, with Jim often barbecuing on a brick barbecue he'd constructed, burning wood he'd collected from hard rubbish. According to Sarah,

> He'd sit on a green plastic chair, tending the fire, cooking the food, and reading a book with his Akubra on. Every now and then he'd softly say 'Ahhh, I love having a fire', which he still says today.

Parenting tactics

Of course, there were unhappy moments too. Jim, who doesn't care or get offended by what other people say to or about him, lacks the understanding that not only do most adults not share this trait, but neither do children; particularly your own children. One particular day Jim was leading a discussion with his young kids about their values, and Jim mentioned that he believed Sarah was the most likely to smoke, drink, take drugs and get into sex work. 'I'm like, "I'm eight years old, Dad, I don't even know what the last one is",' Sarah recalled.

> There are things he said to us as children I will never, ever forget. I'm not angry at him but I have told him, 'Dad, you said these things. Remember you can be wrong. Just because you feel something doesn't mean those judgements are correct'.

When Sarah began a Science degree at twenty-two, Jim told her she couldn't do it because she was 'too emotional'. Today she is studying graduate Medicine and doing very well. 'I'm not too emotional, that's ridiculous. When I was younger, he used to be really critical of my character,' Sarah said. Jim believed Sarah was too concerned with the way people saw her, telling her that her wanting people to like her was 'a critical character flaw', Sarah shared.

I understand why, because once you're trying to please other people there is a lack of integrity, and ... integrity is his thing. But I think most women growing up in our society are concerned with how people see them.

Jim doesn't deny that he pushed his children hard, and explained that he would sometimes describe extreme scenarios to try and scare them straight. 'Sarah has turned out beautifully and I'm proud of her. Plus I didn't say "sex work",' Jim added. 'I just didn't want her to be sexually active, which for teenagers is especially damaging.'

Today, Jim still does the same with his eight-year-old son, Aaron, warning him that good behaviour will be far more difficult in a few years' time. As for his parenting nowadays, Esther, his fourteen-year-old daughter, said,

> He bases his entire parenting on love and discipline, and he's very against overprotection. If I want to go to a party, he doesn't question 'Where's the party? What are you going to do?' He trusts us.

Sylvia, his sixteen-year-old daughter, said something similar:

> I'm glad that [my parents] trust me enough to let me make decisions on my own, but I also know they're there if I need help with decisions. It's really good; they don't force their opinions about my decisions on me.

According to Esther,

> [Dad's] pretty hard on grades. He won't look at the grade, he'll look at the average of the class, and if you're in the average that's not good enough, you need to be above. Though he doesn't really scold us, it's more to scare us.

Andrew and Sarah, Jim's adult kids, spoke very highly of their mother, Felicity. 'She was an exceptionally good mother,' Andrew shared. 'She's a remarkable woman,' Sarah said, adding,

> It's incredible what she dealt with, what she did, and where we are. She's one of the most exceptional people you could ever meet, but it was tough. I know Dad suffered too, but look at his life now. He's got an income, a business, a family, and I don't know he would've done that if he'd had the sole custody of us five children. How could you?

Jim and Felicity's five kids are, across the board, an impressive bunch. The eldest son, Richard, is now living in New York, working at a hedge fund on Wall Street after starting his own successful tech business and moving into Artificial Intelligence through a Master's at Oxford University. The second eldest, Andrew, is studying neuroscience and is also very accomplished in the arts. David is in property and independent game development. Sarah is studying medicine and loving it. The youngest, James, is a very successful lawyer.

In almost all cases, divorces are awful, messy affairs that hurt the parents, and hurt the children far more. 'It was the worst experience of my life,' Jim said. 'I mean, it was more than twenty years ago now, and it still — it's a dreadful hurt. It'll never go away.'

And this divorce was not to be Jim's last.

6

The Jim's Brand Expands

In 1992, amid the pain of divorce, there was still Jim's Mowing to run. Jim worked long days as a distraction, and said his sense of mission and obligation to franchisees was the main thing that held him together during this time. With the business running in five states he held his first national conference in early 1992, near Melbourne Airport.

In 1993 Jim set his sights on New Zealand, the first international expansion. Initially a franchisee from Adelaide volunteered to try, and quickly sold four franchises. But after the initial burst things slowed. He ran out of money, lost heart and came home to Australia. Jim supported those four franchisees from Melbourne but they felt neglected and it was costly. After eighteen months two Melbourne-based franchisees put their hands up to become Auckland franchisors, and after some initial setbacks they did well. Next a husband-and-wife team expanded Jim's Mowing to Christchurch, where within a year they had forty-three franchisees.

After the Wonga Park house was sold Jim moved into a rental at 56 Frogmore Crescent, Park Orchards, one suburb over. He set the office up in the basement, reduced costs and answered the phones himself day and night. It was a sad and lonely time. Sometimes he would walk by the house where his children lived, which was not far away, just to look at it.

In early 1992 a publisher proposed that Jim write a book about Jim's Mowing, which was another welcome distraction. Helped by a professional writer he wrote *The Cutting Edge: Jim's Mowing — A Franchise Story*. It was published in December 1992, but sold few copies. Jim was to update and self-publish many new editions of this book in the years to come, as the Jim's story continued to evolve: in 1999 as *Surprised by Success,* in 2003 as *What Will They Franchise Next?*, in 2013 as *Selling by Not Selling* and in 2016 as *Every Customer a Raving Fan*. In 2018 this was again updated and published as *Every Customer a Fan.* It is available on the Jim's website and Amazon. None of these books sold many copies, and little was done to promote them, but they proved highly successful in a different way.

From the book's first release, copies were given to prospective franchisees and anyone else who showed an interest, 'which helped attract the right kind of people to Jim's; those who value great service to franchisees and customers,' Jim said. Franchisees read it and were moved by his story. Sharon Connell, who would go on to sell over a hundred franchises in three countries, joined Jim's after reading the book. 'Sharon alone would more than justify every cent we spent on printing over the years,' Jim said.

Even while pouring his efforts into the business, Jim never stopped thinking about his research goals. He seized every available day to study and learn, and began rising before dawn and writing in front of the gas fire. From reading research in Primatology, the study of monkeys and apes, he saw that 'animals in limited-food environments showed changes in behaviour, such as delayed mating and stronger pair bonds, that were also characteristic of people in advanced societies,' Jim said. 'It was as if a mechanism evolved to adapt animals to limited food, and that same mechanism made civilisation possible.' In 1992 Jim finished writing his book about his research, *The Hungry Ape: Biology and the Fall of Civilisations.* It was self-published, 'wasn't very good and got very little attention,' Jim said, 'but it helped me work out my ideas'.

New divisions

That same year Jim decided to expand into other services, perhaps cleaning. But his brand was so associated with men doing gardening that he was convinced using the Jim's logo would 'fail dismally': 'I mean the logo is me with a bushy beard in a gardening hat!' Jim exclaimed. 'Who wants a guy like that to clean their house?' He created Sunlite Cleaning, designed a logo and signed two franchisees, but couldn't find them enough work so gave their money back. Then in 1994 a man called John Mahoney approached Jim and proposed using the Jim's brand for a cleaning division and, though sceptical, Jim agreed he could try.

John and Jim became partners for the Victorian rights, with Jim keeping the national rights so he was responsible for the quality of work and the trademarks. 'I needed to ensure Cleaning wouldn't hurt the Jim's brand,' Jim said. When sales reps approached small businesses offering cleaning services, they saw the logo and often responded, 'Oh, *Jim's* Cleaning ... like Jim's Mowing!' John ended up buying

Jim's share of the Victorian rights, and Jim changed the name of his national office from 'Jim's Mowing' to 'Jim's Group' now it was doing more than mowing.

The business soon outgrew Jim's basement, so he rented an upstairs office on the corner of Hawthorn Road and Robinlee Avenue in East Burwood. Anthony Silverman, a franchisee who became a franchisor, described it as a 'dumpy place, it was terrible'. As the business grew they expanded into the vacant offices next door, knocking holes into the walls to join them.

Jim was struggling with the property settlement and child support and couldn't afford a house, so he rented one a few minutes' walk away.

John organised radio ads for Jim's Cleaning, and Mowing franchisees were surprised to find they also received more work as a result. However John's costs soon ran out of control and he wanted out, so Jim bought the business back and ran it from his office, hiring a manager with twenty years' experience in the industry.

By 1995 the office was too cramped and they moved to one in Bayswater, on Scoresby Road. Craig Parke recalled that,

> nothing in the furniture matched, you'd have different carpet, it was all shit. There was actually a bullet hole in our window. A bullet hole in our office window. How the hell did we get a bullet hole in our window?

Again Jim moved to be near the office, this time buying a small house in Bayswater. It had taken him three years since his divorce to afford his own home, though he still needed to rent out rooms to make the mortgage payments. This house was not within walking distance so he cycled each day. 'I absolutely hate commuting,' Jim said. (Today, he lives next door to National Office.)

Craig Parke recalled a dinner Jim hosted at his house around this time. 'No plate, knife, fork or cup matched, and at about 8.30 pm Jim said "I'm going to bed".' Craig recalled.

In October 1995 financial pressure hit again. There had been a great run of three green summers, but most of the franchise sales were now resales or splits (when a franchisee sells off part of their customer base as its own business, echoing how Jim sold mowing rounds in the 1980s). National Office only made 4 per cent from resales or splits (whereas it made 20 per cent of new franchises sold), and the monthly fees, once again, were not covering the office's operating costs. The only thing keeping the Jim's Group afloat was the sale of franchises in new territories.

To survive the financial squeeze Jim cut costs. Some staff even accepted reduced pay, which Jim paid back later. The extra frugality saw the Jim's Group through the summer of 1995–96 and franchisees were looked after, but discontent was growing among the franchisors. They received very little support and no training and resented their fees. However Jim lacked the personal skills to look after them. Though he had built a franchise based on supporting franchisees, he was far less successful at supporting franchisors.

To remedy this he hired a national manager, but when he rang his franchisors to ask if they were being supported well the majority said 'no'. So Jim fired him. Jim advertised the role in Saturday's *Age* and was lucky that one of the four applicants was a man called Peter Hansen, who joined in 1994 as the franchise manager. Peter said, 'When

I joined Jim said, "Peter, I want you to look after franchisors; my role is to look after franchisees"'.

Jim saw that Peter did a good job, but over time tensions rose between them. Peter felt that Jim always sided with the franchisees (whom Jim considered the underdogs of the relationship), and that franchisors needed more benefit of the doubt and support. (Phil Maunder shared the same sentiment: 'He'll always take the franchisee's side over the franchisor's'.) So in 1996 when the rights for New South Wales were put up for sale, Peter bought them. The region was in a bad way, and, with a lot of hard work and stress, 'and not a great deal of help from our friends in Mexico [National Office],' Peter said, he turned it around. 'There was no support.'

Peter Hansen still runs his region today, twenty-two years later, with his son, and though they have sold off smaller regions they currently look after 240 franchisees, the biggest region in Jim's.

With Peter gone, Jim again needed someone to support the franchisors. He asked some franchisors to help him interview candidates, and having their input proved so beneficial that in late 1996 an elected advisory committee of franchisors was created. The committee had no formal power at first, but with time it came to act like an informal board of directors. It would eventually be given control of the branding fund, and the power to approve or veto changes to the manual, something Jim believes is unique in the world of franchising. He sees it as one of his best innovations.

However, the new national manager grew increasingly frustrated in the role and soon left. Over the next two decades a series of people were tried in this role, with some getting fired and some doing well but eventually leaving for better opportunities. Jim sees his inability to locate the right person for this role as one of his greatest failures. 'It wasn't until late 2014 that I found someone who has flourished in the role and helped transform the company,' Jim said.

In 1996 Jim was approached with the idea of a mobile dog washing division, and Jim's Dog Wash was launched with a bright-red logo and its own specially designed trailers. Jim hired a manager with industry experience to run it, and the division grew to seventy franchisees across Australia and New Zealand within seven months.

Jim's Trees started differently. In February 1995 Craig Parke bought a mowing franchise 'for $8000 to $9000,' Craig recalled. He quickly doubled his customer base and, six weeks later, sold a split for $21 000, 'and twelve months later I sold another for the same, so it was pretty good,' Craig said. Craig's next-door neighbour soon bought a franchise, then a neighbour across the road, then Craig's cricket coach. 'Before you know it we're all in it,' Craig said. His mowing customers sometimes asked him to cut back trees, so he got trained and ran a small ad in the paper advertising tree-cutting, but it didn't bring in much work. Craig thought that with the Jim's brand it might, so in late 1996 Craig told Jim, 'We should start Jim's Trees'.

'You start it and see how it goes,' Jim replied. Craig put a small Jim's Trees ad in the paper, 'and we got about three times as many people calling up, plus they were better quality leads with a much higher conversion rate,' Craig said, referring to the percentage of callers that converted to customers. So in January 1997 Jim's Trees was launched, with Jim later offering Craig a job at National Office.

Meanwhile, in 1997 Andrew Mackintosh approached Jim with a proposal for Jim's Fencing. Andrew had purchased a mowing round from Jim in 1988, before it was a franchise, and became a franchisee in 1989. However Jim wasn't keen on Jim's Fencing. The in-house divisions such as Cleaning and Dog Wash were growing but losing money, and he didn't think there would be much demand for fencing. When Andrew persisted Jim agreed to let him do it, provided he owned and ran it himself. Jim's Fencing launched in August 1997, and work flooded in. Today, Jim's Fencing has a higher proportion of unserviced leads than any other division.

Fencing also pioneered a new system of management. The whole division was owned and run by Andrew, so he was highly motivated to make it successful and it made money from the start. From this time onwards, Jim focused on new divisions being owned by the people running them.

In 1999 Jim's Building Maintenance (later changed to Jim's Handyman) was launched in-house, with Jim hiring a manager to run it. Jim's Building Maintenance caused some uproar among the Mowing franchisees, who thought it would cut their lunch; they often did extra jobs for clients that would now fall under the Jim's Building Maintenance division. However the dust settled and they accepted the division, especially when it became clear (as with Cleaning) that different divisions tended to boost the number of mowing leads.

Though launching new divisions was exciting, for the staff at National Office it was mayhem. Katherine Doe, who began working at National Office in 1997, remembers working in accounts, where all the different divisions were set up as separate companies. 'The bookkeeping was crazy,' Katherine said. 'I had to write cheques — there was no internet — between all the companies to cover the shared costs.'

Jim and 'BLEEDING GREEN'

The first division was obviously Mowing, with its famous green uniform, and it's still Jim's biggest division today. Being the first and largest, many franchisors and franchisees over the years have felt great pride for Mowing. As more divisions were launched, some mowing franchisors felt frustrated that all of National Office's effort was no longer on Mowing, the staple Jim's service.

A saying Mowing people often used when other divisions had suggestions about growing Mowing was, 'You don't understand, you don't bleed green'. Even Jim had this attitude to a certain extent. However, despite its use to exclude those who weren't in Mowing, it was, within the Mowing division, a uniting phrase. There was something unifying about Mowing being so in your veins you bled green.

BarterBank

In the mid 1990s, amid the growth of all these new divisions, Jim wanted to explore a side passion of his — trade exchanges. A trade exchange is a platform for the transfer of goods and services without using money. Instead, people or companies trade their goods and services with trade dollars. To be able to start trading, you need to join an exchange, and typically you sign up as a member. BarterCard is one of the best-known trade exchanges.

Jim chose the name BarterBank for his trade exchange, and decided he'd make the fees lower and keep the currency strong 'by not, for example, giving ourselves a huge overdraft,' Jim said. He had the basic software developed and offered people the opportunity of running it. His sister Gill was living in Tasmania at the time with her then husband Andy, and they decided to run it there. 'We worked for two and a half years to build it up from nothing to a multimillion-dollar turnover,' Gill said.

Franchisee Noel Healy was one of the first to join the platform, and he loved the extra work he gained through it. However the problem with trade exchanges is they take a long time to make any money — you need to reach a critical mass of people trading with your trade dollars. It became unsustainable for Jim, and after a few years he sold the exchange. Gill and Andy were left with nothing.

Many years later, in 2014, Jim would make a second attempt, this time utilising the hugely improved technology to build a better trade exchange platform. He called it TradeNet and supported it for a number of years with a handful of employees before ultimately closing it down in early 2018. He explained, 'Unless you give yourself a huge overdraft and basically print money, you just can't make money from it. I couldn't even cover costs'.

National rights

In early 1999 Craig Parke suggested to his brother, Andrew, that he start Jim's Antennas. Andrew was not keen. 'I thought it was a crazy idea,' Andrew Parke said. So Craig started it himself, but Andrew soon bought a franchise, then a regional franchise, and, at the end of 1999, he approached Jim to buy the Australian rights for the Jim's Antennas division. Jim 'literally laughed and said, "you can't buy the Australian rights; there's no such thing",' Andrew recalled. Though Andrew Mackintosh owned and ran Jim's Fencing, having 'National Rights' was new.

Andrew Parke went back to Jim offering a certain amount for the rights, and a percentage for whenever he sold a franchise or a regional franchise, showing Jim how he would maintain the supply of antennas to all franchisees across the country.

Jim agreed, and the first national rights were sold in the Jim's Group, making Andrew Parke the first divisional franchisor in the Jim's system. 'Up until then the divisional franchisor was really Jim. He had some regionals, but no-one looked after the national rights,' Andrew said. 'I think we bought the Australian rights for Jim's Antenna's for $88 000, from memory.' Andrew and his partner spent the next few years flying around Australia 'selling franchises to people in the industry and making sure that their values were in line with ours'. Over the years Andrew continued to build the division, until he sold his divisional and regional rights in November 2016.

North America

By 1996 Jim was considering expanding to North America. Two parties were interested in taking Jim's Mowing to Canada: Trevor O'Donnell, from Australia, and Dennis Reidy, from British Columbia, Canada. Trevor was the franchisor in Geelong, and he sold his region to fund buying the rights with Dennis. Trevor went to Canada for over a year, but returned to Melbourne and Dennis continued running Jim's Mowing there. Dennis did well for a time, but frustrations arose due to pressure from Melbourne to follow Australian systems.

According to Craig Parke, 'Dennis did okay in Canada, but Dennis also hated Jim'. I have contacted both Dennis and his son for an interview, but received no response. Despite the apparent dislike, Dennis Reidy remained the regional franchisor for Jim's Mowing

British Columbia for twenty-one years, selling his rights in early 2018. Joe Badr, a Jim's Mowing franchisee still operating in British Columbia who began in 2000, described it as being very different in Canada, where the brand isn't known like it is in Australia.

The United States had a different beginning. In late 1992 Anthony Silverman, who lived in Melbourne, was ready for a career change. When he gave his resignation, his boss asked, 'What are you going to do?'

'Mow lawns. I want to get some fresh air, exercise,' Anthony replied. A few days later his boss came into work and said, 'Here's a book you might like to read'. It was Jim's book *The Cutting Edge*. Anthony said,

> I read the whole book that night. I put the kids to bed, sat down and started, and didn't go to bed until I'd read the whole book. I was just fascinated.

The next day he rang Jim to organise a meeting, but Jim wasn't available that day so he called VIP. He left the VIP meeting thinking it was a good opportunity, until he met Jim soon afterwards.

At that stage Jim's 'office was in his house, downstairs,' Anthony said. He asked question after question, and Jim showed him everything; a call would come through, Jim would put it in the computer, showing Anthony as he did it. 'He was just an open book,' Anthony recalled with amazement, 'and that's when I realised the big differences between Jim and VIP. Jim is happy to show you everything; "What do you want to see? What do you want to know?"' Anthony bought a franchise.

The next step came in 1995 when Anthony took up the south-east region of Melbourne as a franchisor. In those days franchisors took all the calls themselves, so he set up four phone lines into his house to run the business. 'My wife and I were stuck in the house six days a week answering the phones. We did everything,' Anthony recalled.

In 1996 Anthony wanted to expand his region, and asked to buy the Dandenong and Frankston area, but Jim said, 'No, I'm not selling'. Soon after Jim suggested he and Anthony go for a walk. The office was now in Bayswater and they walked up the street and back. 'How would you like to go to America?' Jim asked. Anthony had never left Australian soil, but he had a thing for American cars. He spoke to his wife, and told Jim 'if you organise visas, we'll go at our expense'.

They decided to launch Jim's Mowing in Dallas, and began preparations. It was arranged that Ron Goldsmith would run Anthony's region from National Office for a small fee while he was away. Jim managed to get Anthony an E2 visa, and in November 1996 the family took off for Dallas, with a stopover in Disneyland on the way.

They instantly hit a road block; the people at the local immigration centre did not know what an E2 visa was and wouldn't give Anthony his Social Security number to be able to work. 'They rang Washington, and eventually found somebody who knew what an E2 visa was,' Anthony recalled. It was the middle of winter in Dallas and all the grass 'looked dead brown,' Anthony said. A neighbour explained that for three months a year the lawns don't need to be mowed, but for nine months you mow weekly. Whereas in Melbourne the average number of 'cuts' per year 'is roughly eighteen, it was thirty-five in Dallas,' Anthony said. This, he realised, would be very lucrative.

Anthony organised a trailer, advertising and got three phone lines running into their Dallas home. Some ads in the local paper brought in plenty of work, and his wife answered the phones while Anthony mowed.

A franchisee from Carrum Downs, Peter Barley, heard of Anthony taking Jim's Mowing to the United States and decided to go too, choosing Houston, Texas. His brother Lewis joined the adventure, and they arrived in Houston and started mowing lawns a few months after the Silvermans had launched in Dallas.

The traditional model for American mowing businesses was one American owner who employed four to six Mexican migrants to do the mowing work. This made it hard to sell franchises: no American wanted to quote jobs and mow lawns themselves; they wanted to employ Mexican workers cheaply to do it.

'We had a lot of trouble finding Americans willing to do the work,' Anthony said. Jim commented that 'one of the nice things about Australia is we're a relatively egalitarian society; there's less of the prejudice against manual labour'. Anthony knocked back thirty potential franchisees, 'because I knew it wouldn't work,' he said. It was frustrating, because the money a franchisee could earn there was great. 'In Australia in '97 the average mowing job was about twenty-five to thirty Aussie dollars. Over there the average job was about thirty-five US dollars,' Anthony said.

In 1997, while Anthony and Peter were mowing lawns in Texas, a big milestone was achieved in Australia. The thousandth franchisee joined Jim's. 'To think I was aiming for a hundred originally,' Jim reflected, grinning. Jim did a media tour as 'the face that launched a thousand trailers', and by the end of 1997 there were over 1350 Jim's franchisees.

But by 1999 things weren't going well in the United States. After two years Anthony had only managed to find a handful of Americans who were keen to get behind a mower themselves. Plus, his eldest daughter was now seventeen and with a steady American boyfriend; he didn't want to stay long enough for her to decide not to come home. On top of this, Anthony had heard that his region in Australia was not being run very well. So it was on his mind to move back home when he got a call from Jim:

'You need to come home, or sell your region,' Jim said, characteristically blunt.

'Why?' Anthony asked.

'Your franchisees are very unhappy with you,' Jim said.

'What do you mean they're not happy with me? I'm paying you to run it; they're not happy with *you*. You're not running it properly,' Anthony replied.

Anthony reflected it was 'typical Jim, throwing it right back at ya'. He was very frustrated Jim blamed him:

They weren't happy because they were treated like crap by National. I don't think — they didn't care. I paid them four grand to take care of my franchisees and they weren't. They were just taking the money, that was easy. When there were problems they didn't want to deal with it, they didn't drive out to the guys, so the guys were frustrated. That's understandable.

Katherine Doe, who worked at National Office for a number of years, explained Jim's call.

By then Jim had an idea of what made a successful franchisor based on what had worked in the past, and he determined that the formula that works best to run a region is having a franchisor who owns it, rather than a paid manager. It mightn't have been so much about Anthony, Jim would have thought, 'It's not working back to the formula'.

Without, unfortunately, thinking through how this felt for Anthony.

Peter Barley hadn't sold any franchises in Houston, but having never been a franchisor this was understandable. When Anthony knew he was leaving Dallas he rang Peter to ask if he wanted to move to Dallas to support Anthony's five franchisees. He did, and Anthony just gave him the business he'd built up.

In December 1999 Anthony and his family caught a plane home. The Jim's Mowing expansion to the United States had been tested, and failed. It was 'incredibly frustrating' for Anthony that the Jim's franchise didn't take off, but, on a personal level, he and his family had had a blast.

Anthony took control of his region again, visiting all his franchisees and fixing the accumulation of problems. While in the United States his calls had been diverted to National Office, and in that time they had changed the phone system, so 'they weren't able to split it off and give me my section back,' Anthony said. National Office kept taking his calls for the next eight months while they sorted it out. 'But by then I didn't want it back,' Anthony said. 'I realised I had freedom, no longer having to make sure someone was always home. Having a central call-centre made sense.' And that is how, in August 2000, the Jim's Group centralised call centre began.

7

The Jim Way

By 1998 Jim had sold off parts of his Victorian mowing region, while keeping the remainder for himself. But he realised his own area was doing poorly, with franchisees feeling unsupported. By contrast, franchisees in regions with regional franchisors (who owned the business) were much happier and growing faster. It was clear the personal responsibility franchisors felt meant they did a far better job than the managers he'd employed to run his regions.

The obvious solution was to divide up and sell the rest of the Victorian mowing rights as regions — businesses — in themselves, 'but this was a scary thought,' Jim said. It would mean losing most of his income, since at the time the monthly national fees were only 15 per cent of turnover; not enough to keep National Office going long term. The only reason he had sold regions in the first place was a desperate need for cash after his first divorce. To make matters worse, his best franchisees didn't have enough cash to buy the regions outright. They would pay it off slowly out of a percentage of profits made by the regions — profits that Jim currently received 100 per cent of. Financially, it looked like a bad decision. 'But in the end it was a matter of core values,' Jim said. 'If I really believed in putting franchisees first I had to do what was best for them.'

Jim's remaining Victorian franchisor rights were quickly bought up, and Jim transitioned out of being a regional franchisor. Now he was only involved with National Office.

Victoria was carved into twenty regions through this change. 'Melbourne had four regions and ended up with ten. If they'd known what they know now they never would have broken Melbourne up into more than maybe eight. I think that was a mistake, making so many,' Anthony Silverman said. Some of the franchisors had to still work on the tools as a franchisee a few days a week to earn enough, which is possible in the Jim's system.

Today many franchisors do this and think it works well, explaining they can bond with their franchisees far better if they're still on the tools themselves. However, some franchisors feel strongly that you shouldn't be allowed to do both. 'You can't be one of the boys,' Anthony told me. 'The day I bought my region, even though I only had thirteen franchisees, I stopped mowing.' As a franchisor there are times you have to be tough, making sure franchisees follow the system. As Anthony said,

> Some make more money as a franchisee than a franchisor — so where is their focus? Are they really being a great franchisor if they're worrying about running their own franchise?

Those who do both say yes. They say they are able to focus on both jobs well, since their franchisees don't take up all their time. Damon Currie is the Jim's Mowing franchisor in Darwin, and he also works on the tools. As he explained, 'There's only five of us here. I'm the franchisor-franchisee so I only handle four other blokes. We're in such an isolated area, and all live fairly close together'. He has no trouble being a franchisor and franchisee.

Today the idea of a limited pie slice is still true on the franchisor level, but for franchisees it works differently. Every time they cut the pie up, bringing another franchisee into a region, the amount of work grows. They don't take work away from the others because the extra trailer on the road increases awareness of Jim's in that area, and thus increases the number of jobs over time. 'New franchisees sometimes think, "the other guys might see me as taking work from them", but that's not the case because we have so much work,' Anthony Silverman explained, adding,

> It's never an issue when we put a new guy on. The other franchisees are happy to help out, I've never known anybody to be upset that there is a new franchisee.

Today the Jim's Group simply can't sell franchises fast enough, there are so many unserviced leads waiting for new operators. Jim said,

> We need good people with great character, who will follow up with clients, care about doing a good job, don't want to let people down, and who take pride in doing their job well.

Having franchisors manage the franchisees that used to be in Jim's regions, rather than managers, worked. Jim said,

> Franchisees reported higher satisfaction, leading to faster growth, which in the long run more than made up for the loss of income. It's one of the many cases in which doing the right thing ended up being the best business decision, even though it didn't seem so at the time.

Still, some new divisions failed. Jim learned that the success of a new division had much more to do with the experience and skills of the divisional than anything else. 'Being a good, single contractor is very different from running a successful state or national business,' Jim said. He began selecting divisionals who had already operated a business, and had good management experience.

Divisionals, who look after an entire division, are the primary support for franchisors in their division, and their responsibility is to sell franchisor rights, set up and run the website, and create the manuals and other documents specific to their division. Normally they are people already in that particular business who want to grow it under Jim's brand. 'A business owner who is doing well themselves can absolutely skyrocket their business with our brand,' Jim said.

> Usually the savings in advertising more than pays for the fees we charge. Plus, we are able to get group discounts, and we have the call centre and the franchising systems.

A good example of this is Jim's Glass. In 2013 the interested parties were already running a glazing business in Adelaide, and they commissioned a survey on who the public would prefer to use, including a couple of local operators, O'Brien's Glass (the largest in the country), and Jim's Glass. 'O'Brien's did much better than the locals, but the best response was to Jim's Glass — which at that time didn't even exist!' Jim exclaimed.

The Jim's brand has this power in the marketplace thanks to the familiarity of seeing it on trailers, vans and cars around Australia. When Craig Parke was working at National Office in the late 1990s and early 2000s he became known as 'Logo-Cop', 'because I'd be onto anyone who changed the logo,' Craig said. To fit the logo on their trailers or vehicles many franchisees were cutting the 'Jim's Mowing' off and sticking it elsewhere, which was terrible for the brand. 'Craig made sure their signage was on correctly,' Jim said. It paid off more than they ever realised it would. Today, though Craig is not involved with Jim's, when he sees a Jim's trailer he still checks 'to see if it is branded properly'.

Jim's way or the highway

In 1997 seventeen-year-old Katherine Doe applied for an admin job at Jim's Mowing, expecting to be helping a franchisee run their business. Instead, she found she'd applied for a job with the Jim's Group office itself in Bayswater. Her filing task in her first week was so monotonous she almost quit on the Thursday, but she pushed through and ended up spending a number of years in various roles at National Office. Later she worked for Jim's Antennas, had her own Dog Wash franchise for a year, and then worked for Jim's Cleaning before setting up her own marketing business for the trade and construction industry.

As a teen in the office Katherine saw habits Jim had that she found surprising in a CEO. Rather than a 'Wash Your Dishes' sign like so many companies have in the office kitchen (and that only a minority of employees listen to), Jim had set up a roster, 'and he was on it,' Katherine said.

> And I'm almost positive, unless I made this up to embellish it one day, that Jim happened to be rostered on the day we had our Christmas party, so he had to clean up the kitchen.

Jim's lack of social graces was also very apparent to staff, due to other odd habits. According to Craig Parke, who worked with Jim for many years,

> It would not be uncommon for someone to be speaking to Jim at his desk, and him to pull out a toothbrush and start brushing his teeth, or clipping his nails. From memory I think he has always cut his own hair, albeit not at his desk during a meeting.

However Phil Maunder did remember this happening on occasion.

> He'd cut his own hair while he was sitting in his office ... He would get a pair of scissors, lean back, pull up the waste paper basket from the floor and cut his hair right there. Or he'd cut his fingernails at his desk, with everybody there.

Another thing Katherine noticed was that roughly every six months Jim would sit in a different team, 'and he would just watch and listen,' she said.

> Jim is really good at taking a part of the business and idealising how it should be, and then putting things in place to try and make it happen. Sometimes [change happened] a little quickly for everyone, but the end result was a direct change.

While Katherine was working in the call centre, Jim sat with them for six months, implementing a number of improvements to their systems and processes. Katherine recalled,

> I think he must have been through the McDonald's drive-through and noticed a buzzer goes off if the customer has been waiting too long. I remembered him telling that story and then he introduced the same thing in the call centre; if the phones had been on hold for too long they would beep and all the managers would know they had to jump in and help.

Jim had developed the habit of answering calls himself whenever there was an overload back in the 1980s, before he franchised.

Valerie Lobo, who has worked at Jim's since 1998, said,

> our system back then was very basic. If you finished a call it lit up with the next and you'd pick it up. If you were on a call and the line was ringing, Jim would pick up.

Her first impression of Jim was both of his social awkwardness and the fact that he was hands on. 'I didn't think he would be in the office taking calls. Things that he can do, he does,' Valerie said. 'But he wasn't a very good call-taker.' After a call they had to manually allocate the job, 'and sometimes he would say, "Ahh I don't think I've done this right". Jim wasn't good at that,' Valerie laughed. At the time the franchisees called the office to put in their work requirements for the next day or week, something they now do online. 'When Jim picked up the phone they used to get really awed that they had Jim on the phone,' Valerie remembered, laughing,

> It was the same with the clients. It used to frazzle them when he said, 'Jim here'. They didn't know if it was *Jim* or who. He would say, 'Yes, yes, I'm the Jim with the beard, the same Jim that you see on the trailer'. It was really hilarious.

In the late 1990s Jim noticed that though he took, on average, 3 per cent of calls, he was responsible for logging roughly 10 per cent of calls making complaints. 'I talked to the staff and realised that their idea of a complaint was different to mine,' Jim said. He asked his staff to log every case of poor service as a complaint, as well as follow-up queries — even if the client wasn't unhappy. Overnight the number of complaints logged soared. 'There were a lot of client complaints about people not being on time or not calling the client,' Katherine remembered.

'I got quite upset,' Jim said. 'I hate customers receiving poor customer service. We were getting far too many complaints.' He addressed this by making all franchisees with excessive complaints call the office every day to put down for work, instead of weekly as was normal. But both franchisors and franchisees protested heavily. Jim asked the franchisors for their suggestions to reduce complaints, and they put forward the idea that every franchisee complaint should be sent to their franchisor, so they were across the complaints and could step in to rectify things. This was put in place.

Complaint uproar

Katherine, working in the call centre at this time, recalled what happened next. Jim proposed a rule that no franchisee should get more than two complaints a year, which the franchisors at the advisory committee accepted. 'And then, being Jim, instead of a slow, drawn-out process,' Katherine explained, this new rule was immediately programmed into the Franchise Management System (FMS). 'The next minute all the franchisees that were over that limit had been what we called "Zedded",' Katherine said, 'which means they couldn't receive any more work outside their territory. And it would've been around 25 to 30 per cent of all franchisees'.

As you can imagine, there was a massive uproar and Jim relaxed the standard so that far fewer franchisees were affected. 'But fast forward two years, and the complaints had gone down drastically,' Katherine said. (Today, a warning letter is sent if a franchisee receives six or more complaints or poor surveys in six months, amounting to at least

6 per cent of leads taken.) It was a good example of how Jim works. Katherine added:

> He'll see something, fix it, cause a massive uproar, but then in the long term it's usually better. In a franchise system it is typically hard to enact change because everyone wants to look after their little patch. They don't see the bigger picture. Jim was often met with opposition, so he had to do it in kind of a rash — well he didn't have to, but he does do it in a rash way. That's how he implements change; he stirs things, but when it settles the change is made.

Nowadays if a client reports any problem, even without actually complaining, a complaint is logged against the franchisee. The same applies with poor survey ratings (the survey system started in 2016). It's the franchisor's job to phone their franchisee and solve the problem and coach them on how to avoid it in future. If necessary the franchisor must visit the customer's home to check out the job. If the client can't be satisfied they are offered an independent report, from an expert agreed to by both parties.

If a franchisee gets six complaints within six months, they are sent a warning letter. If they don't rectify the problem, the next step is a breach notice, and they receive no more work until they've attended retraining. If the complaints continue, they are terminated. Jim is the only person who can delete complaints and bad surveys, and will only do so if there is direct evidence the complaint is wrong, or if the problem has been rectified.

With Jim's sudden change complaints dropped from 5 per cent relative to leads to around 1.5 per cent, gradually falling each year until the survey system was implemented and highlighted more issues. Jim thinks it's no coincidence that the number of leads has skyrocketed in recent years, despite reduced advertising in many areas, and that most franchisees are too busy to take on more work.

'There's really tight quality control in the Jim's Group,' Katherine said. My impression is that Jim wants all his customers to receive excellent service, because it's the right thing to do and it's good for business. He seems to not mind upsetting a small number of franchisees who complain that the process for complaints is too strict, because the greater group of franchisees have an abundance of work because of the good reputation Jim's has, thanks to their great service.

At a training I attended, Mike Davenport, who is the training manager, explained how Jim deals with complaints. 'If you and your franchisor can't fix it, it goes to National Office. And who deals with that?' he asked the audience. 'Jim!' the audience called out. 'And what I take two hours on, he takes five seconds,' Mike told them, saying,

> Where franchisors feel compassion and deal carefully and sympathetically for the franchisee, Jim will see it as black and white: who's right or wrong; done. As much as Jim loves you, he sets a high standard.

Franchisors and divisionals try to make sure issues don't go to Jim; it's not fun being on the other side of Jim's passion and ruthless obsession for great customer service. 'I am very fearful of getting into trouble,' Haydar Hussein, divisional of Jim's Cleaning, said.

> I get nervous when I see Jim. He is like a movie star to me. I get starstruck because I just see him as so smart and intelligent. But I do not want to get into trouble.

Jim and INTELLIGENCE

Jim is a member of Mensa, the oldest and largest high-IQ society. To become a member you take a test. If you pass, it means you have an IQ in the top 2 per cent of the population. Jim took the test many years ago and only just failed, so he had another go and passed. He was adamant that the fact he is a member of Mensa not be shared in this book, but when I said it would be he sighed and said,

Well, if you do write it, make sure you say I failed the test the first time. And if you think of it, I mean all it says is that I'm in the top 2 per cent of Australia's population. We have roughly twenty-four million people, so that means I have the same IQ as roughly 500 000 ... 480 000 Australians. It's not a big deal. I don't like to talk about Mensa because people over-emphasise brains. Brains are not in short supply. It's character and a work ethic that are in short supply. Character is what counts. Sure, a bit of brains is helpful, but it's not everything.

His daughter Sarah said Jim is

a prolific reader. Some of my earliest memories are of Dad sitting in a beanbag or a chair, wholly absorbed in a book. The outside world stopped existing to him. He has a mind-boggling wealth of knowledge on a plethora of subjects.

8

Winning the Lottery

After Jim's divorce he was lonely. He missed marriage and especially his children. 'I'd never thought I would get divorced and felt a great sense of shame, and failure,' Jim said. 'I'm very monogamous by nature. I have a temperament that is totally satisfied with one woman, and I don't function well alone.'

After the divorce he continued attending the Mormon Church, which is strongly against sex before marriage. Soon after he met a young Christian woman who attended a different church. 'We did the wrong thing,' Jim admitted, 'which was devastating because it was against my core principles and beliefs'. After confessing in an agonising interview with his bishop, he felt such turmoil and guilt that he left the Mormons and began attending another equally strict church.

There, several months later, he met a young Filipino woman, Vivian (who declined to be interviewed). 'At the time, she seemed the most beautiful woman in the world,' Jim said. He was soon madly in love, but the church did not approve. 'They thought I should go back to

Felicity,' Jim said, and they put pressure on Vivian to break up with him. Desperate not to lose her, he arranged to fly with her to the Philippines to meet her parents, his fear of losing her greater than his fear of flying. 'I'm insane when it comes to love,' Jim admitted. They married in the Philippines in 1993 after knowing each other for just six weeks.

Vivian quickly fell pregnant, and their son, Tom, was born in February 1994. But only a few months into their marriage Jim had a dreadful, sinking feeling that he had made a terrible mistake. 'I thought, "Oh no, what have I done?"'

The intense feeling of love can cause me to act in the stupidest ways. And marrying Vivian was the single worst decision of my life. We were just completely unsuited.

But the idea of being divorced again 'was absolutely horrifying', so he stuck it out.

'She was a young woman who had five very noisy, lively kids taking over her house once a week,' Jim sympathised. And it would have been particularly hard once Tom was born and she was nursing a young baby day and night. 'I am a very forceful character,' Jim admitted. 'I'm strong-willed and impatient and can easily get angry. Vivian is the opposite. You couldn't have two people more ill-suited.'

Of Jim's three divorces, Vivian's was the only one he initiated. 'I'm not proud of how I acted; the breakup was very messy,' Jim said. It took eighteen months for the divorce to come through, happening in late 1996.

Today Jim has regular contact with Tom, though explaining there is

**a certain amount of tension because of what happened in the past.
But Tom is a fine young man: hardworking, principled, and with a
wide range of interests, and we're getting on better with time.**

After separating from Vivian, Jim got to know a young woman who
worked at National Office, Perri. They soon began dating. Jim's
divorce from Vivian dragged on, so Perri and Jim dated for over
a year before the divorce was finalised in late 1996. They married
immediately after, and soon after that Perri fell pregnant.

When Jim's children had their access visits, he dedicated every
second to them, which was no doubt a shock for Perri. At the time,
Jim was unaware of how hard this would have been for her, just like
he was unaware with Vivian. 'I wasn't a perfect husband,' Jim said.

**When we came back from the hospital with our new baby, William,
I was about to head off to play squash when she objected strongly.
Naturally I didn't go, but it's really hard to imagine what I was
thinking at the time.**

Today he understands how hard it must have been for Perri and Vivian
when his other children visited. 'They were young and we had five to
six children completely take over the house one day a week,' Jim said.
But when Perri asked for a divorce, Jim was utterly shocked. 'I liked
being married to Perri, and hadn't expected it. Plus, three times in a
row was such a terrible failure! I really tried to change her mind for the
next fortnight, but couldn't.'

In 1999 they divorced, and Jim's relationship with their son,
William, deteriorated, which he found deeply sad. 'He was a bright,
adorable little kid,' Jim recalled wistfully.

I loved William so much. I used to carry his picture around in my wallet. But unlike the other kids he didn't want to come on access visits, and in the end I just couldn't force him. He's never wanted any form of contact, and I've never seen him since.

Felicity, Vivian and Perri all declined to be interviewed for this book, but Li's account later in this chapter gives some idea of why Jim's first three marriages failed.

After Perri divorced Jim in late 1999 he began looking for someone new. He hated being single. 'I have this extreme desire to couple. I can't think of anything worse than being single,' Jim said. After many months of looking in Melbourne he decided to travel in the hopes of finding someone. He went to China, but had no luck. World Vision invited him to travel to Yunnan to see their work (he was a donor), and on this trip he met a woman. He followed her to Hong Kong for a few days, but the relationship went nowhere.

Meeting Li

In 2001 a woman at National Office, Du, said she had a perfect match for Jim, a Chinese woman called Li. Du said Li was pretty and suggested they go on a date. He was keen, but Li wasn't.

Li had moved from China to Australia in 2000 after a failed marriage. When Du suggested Li meet Jim, Li's divorce had finally come through (in January 2001) and her faith in love was shattered. Yet she was still attracted to the structure and support of marriage, and she wanted to bring her daughter over from China. But when Du said Jim was a businessman, Li didn't want to meet him. She wanted someone decent and trustworthy, and that had not been her experience of businessmen in China.

But Du kept bringing Jim up. 'She felt like we suited each other,' Li said, 'and she was very, very persistent. After a few tries she convinced me,' and a date was set for 20 April 2001. Li nearly called off the date, but then decided to go dressed plainly in a long skirt and with no makeup, which would turn off any businessmen she knew. They agreed to meet at Hughesdale Station, as she was getting the train from the city.

They met on the platform. Jim was wearing 'a very shabby jacket with a grease patch on the elbow,' Li recalled.

'What's that?' Li asked, pointing at the stain.

'Oh, I must have got it when I was cooking for my kids,' Jim replied, never one to care about how he looked.

'What, you cook for the kids?' Li was pleasantly surprised. She explained to me that businesspeople in China have housemaids, and don't cook for their kids,

> So that was very intriguing. And then he took me to his car and it was a very, very shabby, thirty-year-old Volvo, a yellow one. It was like an antique. I had never seen such an old and broken car in my whole life. I thought, 'He's not the businessman sort I know and understand'.

Jim took Li to Chadstone Shopping Centre for a cup of tea and asked her 'a lot of questions' about whether she liked family, and especially kids, which for Jim is essential. Luckily for Jim, Li loves kids. 'I'm very maternal by nature,' she said. She later commented that 'it was more like a job interview than a normal date. But he was very funny and highly intelligent'.

Jim was totally smitten. 'What really struck me was her vitality, a kind of childlike intensity. Her face was totally expressive and she held nothing back.' Her wardrobe plan backfired: Jim thought she looked perfect. He spent the entire date wishing he could reach out and take hold of her hand, which he did only when they shook hands good night.

The next day they had a second date, and as they were walking back to the car Li took hold of his elbow to steer him around a stream of water falling from a shop canopy. He put his other hand on hers and they walked back like that, Jim desperately hoping that she might be the one. 'All I hoped for was a stable marriage, some children and no more divorces,' Jim said. 'I had absolutely no idea how amazingly it would turn out!'

But the next day Jim had to fly to Florida in the United States with Craig Parke to attend a franchising expo. 'I was absolutely devastated,' Jim said, 'there was nothing I felt less like doing. But go I did'. While Jim pined for her, Li told her mother, 'There's no chance'. He hadn't made much of an impression.

Eight days later he returned. They went out that night, and the next day Jim took Li to meet his mother. While there he said something blunt that offended his mother 'and she was quite upset,' Li remembered. 'She was complaining to me, "Look at my son. He doesn't lie. He doesn't even tell a white lie".'

This was a turning point for Li; honesty was the most important quality she was looking for in a husband. 'When people lie, especially in a relationship, it messes up your plan, your future, trust, everything. It damaged my first marriage,' Li said.

If I wanted a husband to do fine-dining, cooking, holidays, movies, our marriage would have failed. Everybody's expectations for marriage are different. He is so honest, I can rely on him. I can plan my future with him.

Jim's honest and blunt truth-telling has caused some funny moments. Garry Lewis, a Jim's Mowing franchisee of twenty-three years, explained that at his ten-year mark he received a hamper of goodies with a 'congratulations on your ten years' note from Jim that included Jim's mobile number. Garry rang to thank him for the hamper. 'And Jim said, "I didn't send it; it was someone else from the department",' Garry recalled, laughing. Jim couldn't remember this specific call, but said, 'It does sound like me — I can't take credit for something I haven't done'.

For Li, marriage was a practical affair. Hearing Jim was honest to a fault made her serious. 'I wanted a family and to get my daughter here,' Li said.

'If she hadn't been at a low point, and with a daughter to bring to Australia, I doubt Li would have considered me,' Jim said.

That Wednesday they were talking and Li said, 'If we get married —'

'There is no *if*,' Jim replied. This was thirteen days and six dates since their first meeting. Jim explained himself thus: 'When passionate I have no sense of caution or reality, I just can't control myself.' And he was utterly crazy for Li. 'She is wonderful. She's so giving, so kind, fun, intense and vulnerable. She just gives with her whole heart, not holding anything back.'

I commented that thirteen days was very quick to decide to marry.

I knew my third wife [Perri] and my first wife [Felicity] for over a year, both ended badly. Time doesn't matter much. I was just lucky. I often tell Li that God made an absolutely perfect woman just for me.

Li shared a similar sentiment. 'My first husband and I dated for so long, and things still went wrong,' she shared. 'My requirements were so little: as long as he doesn't lie. I am capable, I can support myself and my kids.'

I asked Jim what he would say if one of his daughters decided to marry after thirteen days.

'I'd say, "Don't be stupid",' Jim replied instantly, adding,

but I don't think any of my children are that insane. I just … My passion is so extreme. I can't comprehend people who are happy single, I have this desire to bond and spend my life with someone.

There was no pre-nuptial agreement, which most men in Jim's position would insist on. 'I've never had one,' Jim said. 'I refuse to recognise a marriage might fail.'

Jim wanted four essential things in a wife. That she share his love of children; be willing to attend church with him ('She didn't need to be Christian; I just wanted her to come with me,' Jim said); understand his research ('Can't be compromised in any way'); and, finally, be a person of morals. Li met all these criteria beautifully.

When they married on 10 June 2001, seven weeks and two days after their first date, Jim was 'absolutely crazy, really off my head' in love with her. Li liked him 'well enough' but wasn't in love. As she put it, she had lost faith in love when her first marriage broke up.

Li moved into Jim's house in Bayswater, which 'by her standards was pretty crummy,' Jim said.

Li recalled, 'I thought he was very poor when I married him. I remember thinking, "As long as he doesn't touch my money I'll be okay"'.

But 'she was happy to be settled and to get her daughter over from China,' Jim said.

Li quickly fell pregnant and gave birth to Sylvia in March 2002. Which was lucky, because according to Jim

There were times she got so mad at me she went away for a few days. Luckily, being pregnant at the time kind of held her in!

The following year they managed to bring Li's daughter from her first marriage, Jasmine, to Australia. Jasmine was four, and Jim gladly adopted her as his own. 'We think of each other as father and daughter, the word "step" never comes into it,' Jim said.

Li found the beginning of their marriage tough, with seven lively kids invading the house every weekend and Jim being totally focused on them. It was the same problem that had ended his last two marriages. But Li was great with the children. 'She loved them as her own, and would have gladly adopted them if that had been possible,' Jim said. She also greatly appreciated his obvious love for Jasmine.

Still, she found the first two years of their marriage very hard. She just couldn't understand him, and often found him 'very annoying'. Jim could see her frustration and loved her a lot, but couldn't be anything but himself. He was aware she hadn't married out of love, despite his love for her, and hoped she would come around.

In the beginning Li kept trying to change Jim, challenging his decisions to invest so heavily in different areas that to her seemed too risky. Her efforts to change him were met with anger. A comment from one of Li's friends, suggesting Jim might have Asperger's, helped Li understand his behaviour. Jim has never actually been tested or diagnosed, but the new perspective helped Li change her own behaviour. In the end, she made a choice.

I said to myself, 'Do you love this man? Yes, I love him a lot. I respect him. And he was successful before he met me, so I can make it better, but I must let him be himself. If you love this man and he's so upset with you getting involved in what he wants to do, it's not worth it'.

Jim described this turning point:

She stopped trying to make me change and just did whatever needed doing, and I responded, giving back. Sometimes I have to physically pull her away from the sink to stop her washing up, or insist on picking up one of the children late at night when she's tired.

Li commented that

He changed. Even the staff in the office said he changed a lot. When I married him he was very self-centred, but not anymore. He does lots of things for me; like he does the bed, not because he likes it but because he knows it will make me happy.

Li described Jim as

socially awkward and very misunderstood…His love for his franchisees is just amazing. They only see his tough side. He cares a lot, just nobody sees it. His passion and love for his franchisees is unbelievable. When a franchisee fails, for whatever reason, I can feel the pain from him — after the conversation on the phone, where he has to be strong and has to do the right thing, he will make comments that show he's hurt by it.

A honeymoon marriage

When I asked Jim what the most important events in his life over the past twenty years have been, I expected him to talk about his research, or the Jim's Group expansion. It was neither:

Meeting Li in 2001. That was absolutely life changing, and it has shaped every day of my life for the better. Nothing else comes even close to that, quite frankly.

Jim described their marriage as a 'seventeen-year honeymoon', though Li sees it more as a 'fifteen-year honeymoon'. In the words of Sylvia, their sixteen-year-old daughter, 'My parents are so affectionate it's kind of disgusting'.

'We're very lucky we met,' Li said, although 'he still annoys me a lot; Jim has a very difficult personality'.

Jim reflected that he

couldn't have found a better wife if I looked for a thousand years. I won the lottery when I met her. She's a great mother and a wonderful business partner, and has helped me in so many ways. It's uncanny. How could anybody be so perfect? I'm crazy about her; the honeymoon never ends.

Every year on 20 April they go back to Hughesdale railway station to celebrate the meeting that transformed both their lives.

9

Growth

In 2000 Jim's Group included Mowing, Cleaning, Dog Wash, Trees, Fencing, Carpet Cleaning, Car Cleaning (later changed to Car Detailing), Blind Cleaning and Repairs, Antennas, Building Maintenance (later changed to Handyman), Bookkeeping, Paving, Mobile BBQ, Security Doors, Wardrobes, Alarms, Motor Vehicle Repair Service, Floors, and Road Training. The last seven are not in operation today. Those who were franchisors at this time look back with nostalgia and a smile, or a grimace of frustration because they wish things were still the same.

'Back then we were what you might call less regulated,' said Jason Jaap, who was a franchisee, then franchisor, then expanded Jim's in the UK.

> The contracts were very vague, and we pretty much did what we wanted to some degree. We loved the business back then, we lived and breathed it, and we made good money.

Andrew Parke shared the same sentiment, remembering the great friendships all the early guys had:

> We were all learning from each other and sharing ideas. Jim was very much, 'You've got the rights, do what you have to do'. There wasn't

a lot of support from the office; we had our own little group that tended to come up with the right way of doing things ourselves.

Craig Parke said that around 1999 to 2004 were 'the golden years'.

We went to each other's weddings — it was the good times... There was lots of growth and money being made, lots of development, lots of banter, lots of fun.

For Phil Maunder,

the good old days were from about 1990 to about 1997, and then things started tightening up. Jim started to employ other people in the business and the control tightened... We were dictated how to run things and what we were meant to do.

I remember in the early days there was a state franchisor who, according to Jim, didn't do the right thing. Jim... was quite ruthless because the guy wasn't performing and wasn't looking after his franchisees according to Jim — whereas if you did the right thing... you were left alone to run your business, which I enjoyed.

Greg Puzzolo, one of those Jim employed who helped tighten things, recalled the golden years as being from 1998 to 2007.

Garry Lewis became a Jim's Mowing franchisee in 1994, and stayed until he retired twenty-three years later. 'It was different back then. You would just go out with another guy and if he determined you capable of mowing a lawn, you could start the next day.'

According to Anthony Silverman,

In the early days Jim was kind of a different person; you could come up with ideas, everyone was trying stuff. We would pass ideas among ourselves and Jim was part of it. It was all encouraged, but something somewhere changed.

It is clear those early franchisors played a big part in the early growth of Jim's. When Phil Maunder took Jim's Mowing to Adelaide, he did everything, as is true for those who expanded Jim's to the other states and countries. Jim was there on the other end of the phone when they rang, but ultimately they used his brand and system and made a success of it themselves. And many didn't — but they would sell out to others, who then usually did. 'I'd really [attribute] his success to people like me and others expanding outside of Victoria,' Ron Sadowski said. 'His concept was brilliant but it needed refining. We did our own marketing.' Jason Jaap had a similar sentiment.

> Jim'll tell you this himself; a lot of his successes are based on the people he had around him. He had a lot of good people, including some of the people who worked for him directly, as well as his franchisees and franchisors.

An experimental attitude

Jim was always happy to try new ideas. 'Jim always asked us to try something, anything, just keep trying different things. And if it didn't work you try something else,' Peter Hansen recalled.

Brendan Hill, an employee of fourteen years, said, 'I think the whole experimental attitude, in the long term, does work. Every now and then he hits on something that does phenomenally well'.

Stuart Lewien, who has worked at National Office since August 1993, said,

> It's nice he's open to try out so many new things; it means that we get to do some really exciting stuff. Literally [starting] last week...we are able to work for 10 per cent of our time on things we think will most benefit Jim's, as a trial.

Peter Hansen said, 'He established that as a small business you could be nimble, agile, whereas these days [National Office is] like a government department'. He sighed, frustrated with how controlled things are today. 'He doesn't really want creativity, as much as he'll tell you he does. It's gotten to a point where they tell us what we can do.'

Anthony Silverman agreed, remembering back to the early days when 'Jim was really good at saying, "That worked, that didn't work", and encouraging us to try stuff. You can't do that anymore, it's a little frustrating'.

Many of those early guys were very entrepreneurial, and it shows in what they are doing today. Jason Jaap, Phil Maunder, Craig Parke and Andrew Parke all run their own thriving businesses today, and Ron Sadowski and Anthony Silverman are still successful Jim's franchisors.

However those unregulated 'golden years', that saw so much growth and expansion and were filled with camaraderie, had to come to an end. Said Jason Jaap,

> It was Jim, with the help of the managers around him, that realised the business needed to be restructured, and I guess that decision played a large part of where he is today. Contracts had to become tighter.

Jim saw it in much the same way.

> Most franchisors genuinely cared about their people and tried to do the right thing, but controls were very loose. When we went looking for contracts they were often missing, or didn't define a territory properly. Some franchisors were pocketing or misspending the

marketing money. Or taking far more than the allowable 20 per cent from a franchise sale …

We not only stopped the abuses but in many cases compelled franchisors to make refunds. Customer service was also highly variable, with many franchisees failing to get coached with regard to complaints, and many trailers a disgrace. To put it mildly, tightening up on this did not always make us popular.

We also had to provide much better support to franchisors ourselves, which over time we did.

Jim and CREATIVITY

One of Jim's strengths, which is often overlooked, is his creativity. Jim's lawyers said he comes up with solutions they hadn't thought of. Richard Long, one of Jim's programmers, explained how the team would be stuck on a problem all morning, and then Jim would poke his head in to see how they were going, and instantly come up with a solution. 'Why didn't we think of that?!' Richard said he and his colleagues often wonder.

Perhaps Jim's creativity is overlooked because we often associate creatives as people who have soft and colourful characters, always buzzing with ideas. Jim's abrupt, practical, direct manner does not give off the vibes of a creative — but his creativity in business is extreme.

'I'm not bound by the past, I always look for totally new solutions and approaches. I never do something just because that's the way it's always been done,' Jim explained. 'That's basically what killed my academic career; I was too unorthodox. But in business it often works quite well.'

Jim's Cleaning

In 2001 Jim's Cleaning wasn't doing well. Andrew Parke thought his neighbour, Haydar Hussein, who had his own cleaning business, Cleaners Choice, could make it work. Andrew suggested Haydar join Jim's Cleaning, but Haydar resisted. He had his own business, his own brand, and he'd never even heard of a 'Jim's' anything before. 'I didn't want to "merge" or try anything different — I had my own dreams,' Haydar said.

But Andrew was convincing, so Haydar decided to buy a Jim's Cleaning region. After meeting with Jim and signing the contract he went home — 'And that was it,' Haydar recalled. 'I didn't get anything. No manual, nothing. I expected more.' He rang Andrew Parke asking, 'What do I do?'

Today Jim's has an onboarding process with training and manuals, meetings and phone support. But this was Jim's in 2001. 'In a way it was good because it meant I had to make my own plan,' Haydar reflected, 'my own systems and directions. That is probably one of the secrets of Jim's; we were able to be creative, organic and we built our own systems'.

Today Jim's Cleaning, thanks to Haydar buying the divisional rights soon after and working very hard (and smart) for the past seventeen years, is the second biggest division after Jim's Mowing, with 750 franchisees at the time of writing, including subdivisions such as Jim's Carpet Cleaning and Jim's Car Detailing. 'When I first joined there were only fifteen or sixteen franchisees,' Haydar said, before leaning forward and whispering with a grin: 'a little secret — Cleaning will be bigger than Mowing. We're always looking at what they're doing and doing it better'.

In 2018, for the first time ever, more Jim's Cleaning franchises were sold in a month than Jim's Mowing franchises. This was a big moment. In 2017 Jim's Cleaning alone had 15 000 unserviced leads. In Cleaning they typically advise that a new franchisee can start a great business with twenty-five to thirty leads a month because of the repetitive work and word-of-mouth referrals, which means they have enough work for another 500 franchisees to start tomorrow. 'So, the sky is the limit,' Haydar grinned.

I asked how much an average cleaning franchisee earns per hour. 'They do $60 to $100 an hour. You wouldn't get $100 consistently, but consistently you would get $60,' Haydar said. I was amazed one could earn so much from cleaning houses, asking, 'Does that mean most of your franchisees are turning over $100 000 or more each year?' He replied that most are.

Of course there is the initial investment to buy a Jim's franchise, the equipment costs and the ongoing fees to take into account. 'There are new Australians who come from a war-torn country turning over $1000 a day in Jim's Cleaning, who, in their own country, were probably getting four cents a day,' Haydar said.

The immigrants' plight is close to Haydar's heart, with his own parents having come to Australia from Turkey with one suitcase in the 1970s. He reflected that forty years ago new immigrants didn't have great job prospects, but with Jim's they do. Haydar said,

> They deserve this opportunity and will benefit from it, and that is what motivates me to keep signing them up. Imagine all the reward I get from helping these families. Some of them have small children, and I help these people become somebody.

I asked Jim about the Cleaning division. He said,

> Haydar shows exactly why it's the leadership rather than the type of job which decides how a division will go. Cleaning was nothing before Haydar took charge and now it's a star. He's an amazing, charismatic leader who inspires others but is always willing to learn. I've learned more from him than he's ever learned from me. He's also decent, caring, totally ethical, and I'm really proud that he's done so well out of Jim's. I often joke that his new house is the only building on the planet that can be seen with the naked eye from Mars. As to Cleaning overtaking Mowing, we needle each other about it but in reality, no-one would be more delighted than me. After all, we each get half the income!

National Office gets its own office

In 2003 Jim's financial situation was, for the first time since his first divorce, looking good. Three more marriages and two more divorces; multiple child support payments; his project in Marysville; BarterBank; and his dedication to pouring any profit back into the business had kept his personal finances at just enough to support a very basic lifestyle. 'I was this supposedly wealthy businessman who drove a decrepit car and wore old clothes and lived in a rather shabby house,' Jim said. 'If you look at my life until 2003 you'd think, "This guy has got no money at all".'

But in 2003 he could finally afford to buy his own building for the National Office. He came across a 20-acre property in Mooroolbark, 30 kilometres east of Melbourne, that had been a girls' school and a university before lying vacant for six years. After gaining permission from the council to turn it into an office and conference centre, he bought the place and moved the National Office in at once.

If you visit today you will find a newly built conference centre and accommodation, beautifully set among gum trees, and a far less new and far less fancy National Office. But when Jim bought it there was no conference centre or accommodation, and the office buildings were in a terrible state.

Shirley Harry, who began working for Jim in 1997 and left at the start of 2018, remembers a funny conversation with one of the call centre girls when they first moved in. Upon arriving, the girl exclaimed, 'I remember this place, I used to go to school here!'

'What was it like?' Shirley asked.

'Not like this.'

Shirley recalled that 'there were rabbits and snakes everywhere, and the place was overgrown'. There was a problem with the plumbing in the office building, so plumbers were called in. The staff were working while the repairs happened, and Shirley remembers someone asking, 'What's that strange smell?' Then in the middle of the office a whole lot of gunk spilled out of the pipe the plumbers were cleaning out.

It wasn't only the plumbing — the electrics were also temperamental. 'I had to keep going out to the fuse box and fixing it, because if we used too many appliances the whole place would trip out,' Shirley recalled. An electrician was called in who fixed the issues and put in safety switches.

For some time spiders, insects and lizards frequented the office, with the call centre girls running outside, squealing, each time. One day a manager cleaned out one of the toilet blocks further down the property, and came back up shouting, 'Look at all these dead snakes!'

Despite its rough beginnings, the 20-acre property is now a beautiful place to visit and work from. Multiple staff members commented that one of their favourite things about working for Jim's Group is the short drive to and from work (rather than getting caught in Melbourne traffic), and the beauty of the property. The surrounding gums and sloping grass and bushland are beautiful, birds call to each other from the trees, and going from one office building to the other is a peaceful, enjoyable walk.

National Office itself is in no way flashy, still in the original education buildings built long ago. Jim has renovated the inside, adding a nicer ceiling, lighting and carpets, but there is no grandeur.

The office is open plan and bright, and everyone has the same functional desk, including Jim. His value of transparency shines through the simple, open layout, and his office door is always open, unless a staff member specifically asks to close it. He has a whiteboard behind his desk that is usually clean, an empty bookcase, and the only personal item is the purple exercise ball he uses as a chair.

After buying the property, Jim hunted for a house within walking distance. Jill Stallworthy, the manager of the Jim's call centre, recalled that 'nothing was for sale, so he knocked on all the doors — he thinks like that. People wait for a "For Sale" sign — Jim didn't'. The owners of the house next door were happy to sell and he bought it.

Jim's garden is an unruly, beautiful mess, something that a number of the franchisors and franchisees made a point to comment on. They love telling new franchisees to 'check out Jim's garden when you're at training, it's spotless!' so the new guys will get a surprise. Most expect the man who built an empire out of gardening and home services to have a manicured place, but Jim loves a wild garden. He spends much time working in it, but he doesn't favour the aesthetic of neat garden beds.

Soon after moving in to their new house Li fell pregnant again, and in June 2004 she gave birth to Esther. Five years later she gave birth to their youngest child, Aaron. Shirley noticed a difference in Jim, thanks to Li. 'He was making more of an effort to actually talk to people, being more social, joking around. She really brought out the best in him,' Shirley recalled. But he still didn't like anyone coming near him, 'which was hysterical most of the time,' Shirley laughed. 'He used to always tell me off when I'd take photos, because I'd say "Closer, closer," and he'd say, "No, that's it".' Shirley laughed again.

Jim's national conferences

The Jim's national conferences began as small affairs. They weren't extravagant, but the franchisors enjoyed seeing each other, talking business and having fun in the evenings. ('We would go party, but Jim wouldn't,' Ron Sadowski said.)

Things evolved through the 1990s and into the 2000s, with more franchisors and divisions joining Jim's, and more exotic conference locations. There were conferences in Sydney, Cairns, the Gold Coast, New Zealand, Oakland, Fiji... at one point, due to the franchisors' requests, a franchisor conference was being held every six months. 'It was crazy; we were always organising a conference!' Katherine Doe recalled. There weren't many other occasions for them to get together in those days, so the conferences were significant. Each had a different theme: there was 'Survivor', where they all built rafts; 'Invent a New Division', where the creativity went to all sorts of wacky and R-rated places; 'Australian Outback', where they danced country and western. 'Poor Jim would say his bit in his greens, he wouldn't dress up and then he'd just go,' Vanessa Parke, Craig's wife, remembered.

One time it was an 'Arabian Nights' theme and the staff convinced Jim to ride a camel and, though he went along with it, a photo taken on the night shows he didn't love the experience (although he hates smiling in photos at the best of times).

Another year, as part of a deal Optus had with the Jim's Group they sponsored a conference, 'and we finished the deal and got this surplus money that had to be spent on that conference,' Katherine Doe recalled. 'It was a crazy amount of money.' The conference was on the Gold Coast, so they booked out the whole of Sea World one night, and the whole of Movie World the next night. 'We always tried to make the conferences be for everyone. The Jim's businesses are family businesses,' Katherine said.

Jim always brought his family to the conferences, something his wife, Li, remembers fondly, taking out her phone and showing me photos of when they were on the Gold Coast. When I asked franchisors if they ever saw the family man side of Jim, Anthony Silverman said, 'At conferences he would sit with his kids — he loves his kids, he's very family oriented. But when he's at work he's all about business'. Paul Sandles of Jim's Diggers said, 'Jim's quite shy, so at conferences he wouldn't normally get too involved'. (This is in sharp contrast with the central role he plays at franchisor dinners, discussed in chapter 11.)

Jason Jaap remembers that Jim 'was always gone by 9 pm. He wasn't a very social person. His social skills were never the best but he is a very good public speaker, particularly when talking about his business'.

However, Jim wasn't always up for big crowds. At a conference on the Gold Coast Greg Puzzolo, who was CEO at the time, organised the first three-hour session of the conference to be a 'This Is Your Life' about Jim. Greg had the okay from Jim and had photos and questions prepared. But the night before Jim rang Greg.

'Sorry Greg, I'm leaving,' Jim said.

'Leaving where?'

'I don't want to be here.'

'But Jim, this is your conference, your business,' Greg said, exasperated.

'I'm leaving.'

Greg had no idea what to do to fill the three hours the next morning. He rang Andrew Parke and said, 'I'm stuffed mate'. Andrew and Greg sat on the couch drinking 'a bottle of bourbon or something,' Greg recalled, and a number of drinks down Greg said — 'Joe Kerlin is a ventriloquist. Let's bring up Joe's dummy, dress it up as Jim, and do the session!' And that's exactly what they did.

'We got better answers from the doll than we would have from Jim!' Andrew recalled, laughing.

Ron Sadowski recalled a conference in the early days when there were still only about eight guys. Ron was sitting next to Peter Hansen and Phil Maunder and they were all laughing and joking. At one point Ron, friends with everyone and always ready with a joke, turned to another guy saying, 'G'day, pal. How're you going?' Out of the blue Jim interrupted, looking straight at Ron and saying, 'Ron, I've got no friends'.

'The room went silent. Seriously, silent,' Ron recalled.

And I said, 'Jim, I'm your friend'. And Jim actually came back years later and said, 'Ron, I class you as a friend. I haven't got many, but you are one'. He's just a very sensible, straightforward man, not hugely humorous. But he's good, I like his company.

Vanessa Parke, Craig's wife, only got to experience Jim at the conferences, and when I asked her how she would describe him, her first word was 'generous'. 'At conferences the wives always got pampered with different things — spas, massages — he was always generous.'

Things changed when the Foothills Conference Centre was built next to National Office and the conferences could be hosted there, ending the excitement of flying to different locations. I attended the July 2018 national conference and gala dinner, hosted at Foothills. The conference was both educational and entertaining, with useful information sessions: Kevin Sheedy as the guest speaker; and an afternoon session with Jim, Tino Grossi (at that time CEO) and operations staff member Joel to answer any questions people had. For the gala everyone got changed out of their Jim's uniforms and into fancy attire — everyone except Jim, of course. Jim's wife, Li, attended, looking fabulous, but their kids didn't come. Aaron and Sylvia stayed home, and Esther was working for Foothills as a waitress that night, serving food and drink to the franchisors and divisionals in her Foothills uniform. She had told me a few months earlier that she couldn't wait to be old enough to get a job — now she was.

The evening began with an entrée while all the awards were given out, which took a good hour. What stood out was that most awards were for service to franchisees, as measured by the franchisee survey. The last five minutes were spent giving awards for growth: the only awards incentivising sales.

Foothills Conference Centre

When buying the 20-acre Mooroolbark property in 2003 Jim's idea was to have accommodation on site, so prospective franchisees and franchisors could stay during training. The property had plenty of buildings, far more than needed for offices, but only two small houses for accommodation. Unfortunately, financial difficulties (discussed in the next chapter) made him briefly consider selling the property. It would be five years before the first accommodation units were built, in early 2008.

Jill Stallworthy from the call centre and Valerie Lobo from National Office worked with the builder on those units. Once built they needed furnishing, and quotes came back at around $200 000. Li was astonished at that cost, 'for twenty-four rooms!' she exclaimed. She knew she could find much cheaper good-quality furniture in China, and went over there to source furnishings, completing the project for $50 000. 'The beds are so good guests sometimes ask where they can buy them!' Jim said. After sleeping there myself I can attest to that.

In September 2008 the doors of the Foothills Conference Centre opened, and in April 2009 the Jim's Mowing Conference was held there for the first time. Soon after another thirty rooms were built, and the next year the conference centre was renovated. In its first year Foothills had a string of managers and lost money, with the last manager quitting in late 2009. Four months earlier Li had given birth to their son, Aaron, but Jim still asked if she could step in to run it. Li's aunt, mother and sister helped with Aaron so she could take it on. 'I knew nothing about running a conference centre,' Li laughed. She learned on the job, hired a great head chef and events manager, and got the business out of the red and making a profit in her first year at the helm.

Jim had always wanted Foothills to have near one hundred rooms so it could host national conferences, and he had plans drawn up to build more rooms. Li didn't like the plans, so she designed 42 stylish rooms around an open square with a garden and fountain in the middle. Jim approved, so she set to work managing the construction. The finished result is beautiful.

Li continues to run Foothills, though these days she spends most of her time on her successful construction business. Jim is her mentor in business. 'He helps me a lot. I get discouraged,' Li said. 'If I lose money I get really upset. He doesn't. He never doubts himself. I really admire him for that.'

Today the Foothills Conference Centre has ninety-six rooms, two lecture theatres and multiple conference rooms that can host up to 300 people. A wood-fired pizza restaurant has been opened, and plans are currently with the council for a sporting complex containing a gym, heated pool and racquetball court.

10

Business Can Be Tough

From 2001 to 2003 seventeen new divisions were launched: Roofing, Window and Pressure Cleaning, Electrical, Computer Services, Pool Care, Test and Tag, Painting, Sand Soil and Gravel, Appliance Repairs, Balloons, Beach House, Preggi Bellies, Irrigation, Concreting, Garden Edge, Marie's Mobile Hair, and Pool Care Retail. The latter ten divisions are not in operation today.

'In those days we had rather more failures than successes,' Jim said.

> We signed people who had a good idea and were running a successful one-man business, but without staff or management experience. After that, we only took on people with a proven track record. It was clear that the quality of the founder mattered far more than the type of service.

Since 2005 the Jim's Group has started forty-one divisions with only eight failures (Windscreens, Graffiti Solutions, Bathrooms, Concrete Cutting, Insulation Services, Driving School, Site Solution and Timber Milling).

The impact of most division failures wasn't severe, with little investment by the founders and few, if any, franchisees signed. But Beach House Fitness Centres (a health club), caused a lot of damage.

Fiascos

Beach House was a big investment because they needed a physical location to operate. Some Mowing franchisors decided to buy a franchise in the new venture, and Li, who'd had her money from China brought over, did too.

'I got involved in Beach House, and it failed badly,' Li said. 'Everybody — the franchisor and us — all failed.' They all lost their money, with some even losing their homes and having to declare bankruptcy.

This was an extreme case of a division failing. For those who went bankrupt, which terminated their regional franchisor's rights, Jim simply granted their region back to them as a rental on the same terms. This meant they retained their core asset and could build themselves back up. 'The Jim's Group is pretty tribal, and I put my franchisors way ahead of any creditors,' Jim said.

Jim sees the Beach House fiasco as one of his worst failures because of the damage it did. 'I didn't lose anything, but some of my best people, plus Li, were basically wiped out,' Jim said.

We didn't understand the business and left it in the hands of our partners, which was a mistake. The business model wasn't properly worked out, which we only realised too late. Since then we have stuck to businesses where franchisees service clients onsite, something we understand very well. We'll never do anything like Beach House again.

Another fiasco was when an accountant left, after which Jim said he received

> a $3 million bill from the ATO for back taxes, penalties and interest, and I have *never* been involved in tax evasion before or since.

Jim's attempt to track this down and pursue the accountant and another terminated manager was abandoned. 'It would have cost too much,' Jim said.

The tax bill meant that Jim's plans of building a conference centre next to National Office had to be delayed.

I asked Jim what he felt, receiving a bill of $3 million. He replied, 'In terms of pain, not seeing my kids six days a week was a ten out of ten. The $3 million bill was a two out of ten'.

When Beach House had failed, Jim had helped Li. Li said,

> He paid the lawyer's bill, sorted it out and we managed to give the business away to someone who made a big success out of it. Jim was happy to get me out of the trouble, so I felt like I owed him.

After the accountant resigned the accounts department was in shambles, and Li stepped in to manage it. In China Li had been a teacher, then worked in tourism, and her last job was with 'the British Consulate General in Chongqing, my city,' Li said. 'So I had a bit of experience. I'm not a bookkeeper nor an accountant. It was just common sense.' For example, she found that they were still paying for a service that had stopped five years before.

'Nobody bothered to check, only me because I have the owner's interest at heart,' Li explained. She also found that many debts were being written off without any written authorisation. 'Where's the paperwork? Where's the trail? You can't just write off somebody's debt,' Li said, exasperated. In 2005 she put in place processes and systems to prevent the needless loss of money, and then hired a good accountant. Today, if the finance team have been told to write off a debt, they have to check with Li before doing so (unless the order comes straight from Jim himself). Jim spoke glowingly of the work Li did. 'She's never studied accounts, and she sorted out the finance department, which back then was a mess. She's just brilliant.'

Referendum

At this time another issue was brewing. Many franchisors felt Jim was getting in the way of them running their businesses, and in 2005 this deep dissatisfaction came to Jim's attention. 'I was pushing very hard at this time for better service to customers and franchisees,' Jim recalled. 'But not being at all social, I had no idea how badly they were taking it. Also, our communication of changes was poor.' There was talk of a group challenge, with funds being collected for a joint legal case.

Jim responded by calling a referendum, giving franchisors the opportunity to vote him out. 'He put himself in the firing line,' Jill Stallworthy, manager of the call centre, said. She recalled him saying, 'If I get voted out, I'll walk'. Anthony Silverman remembered 'a lot of franchisors ringing up other franchisors saying "you need to vote him out"'.

There was a vote: did they want new leadership, or for Jim to stay at the helm? Would the Jim's franchise run more successfully with or without him?

It was Jill who had the job of counting the votes. 'It was in his favour,' Jill said, and Jim remained in charge. 'At the end of the day it's the franchisors' financial investment too,' Jill explained. 'Better the devil you know than the devil you don't. Obviously, a lot of them realised that.'

Jim and HIS TEMPER

Jim has a temper that can instantly flare: 'I get very emotional about customer service. It's not a rational thing, I'm just over-the-top emotional about it.' Numerous franchisors, past and present, shared stories of Jim erupting in meetings. Jim readily admitted he does.

I get angry at people when I shouldn't … I always feel bad afterwards. I'm not tactful, I wish I was. When I'm angry with a franchisee about customer service, what am I achieving?

He then shared that the day before, Tino Grossi had called about a matter that in the moment Jim had misunderstood, and he'd erupted in the middle of the office. 'I was absolutely furious. I started ranting and yelling, "Why are we doing this?!"'

Later that day Tino called Jim to explain the situation properly, and Jim realised he was in the wrong. Tino also told Jim that his behaviour wasn't good, particularly in the middle of the office. Jim apologised to Tino on the phone, then

I wrote a general apology to all the staff saying my behaviour was inexcusable. Even if I had been right, it didn't justify it. And this morning I wrote to my team telling them to let me know if I do something stupid like that again, because I really appreciate the fact Tino told me.

Jim added, 'Losing your temper at somebody is bad when they've got less power than you — it's not so bad when they've got more'.

The stories I heard from past franchisors of Jim losing his temper didn't include apologies like this; it seems to be something he has learned more recently.

UK struggles

A few attempts had been made over the years to grow Jim's Mowing in the UK, but it hadn't worked very well, perhaps due to cultural and climate differences, or because it was tricky to provide proper support and adequate training from Australia. Or maybe the right person simply hadn't tried it yet. In 2003 Jason Jaap thought he might give it a go.

Jason's involvement with Jim's started in 1992, when he became a Jim's Mowing franchisee at twenty-one after seeing an ad that highlighted an $800 per week work guarantee. Jason met with Jim at his office, which was then at the back of Jim's house in Park Orchards.

> He had a self-made call centre out the back and it was a bit shonky, but it seemed to work pretty well. He didn't care much about the furniture or the material things so to speak, it was all about the customer service for Jim.

Jason signed up, later becoming a franchisor. He always thought Jim's would be a stepping stone for him to learn about business. 'I didn't do a degree in business; I learned from working for myself in the Jim's environment,' Jason said. His main lesson was the importance of great customer service.

> If you put aside Jim's faults — and I think he'll tell you there were a few, and I won't deny that — one thing he is passionate about, and is very good at, is customer service. That has put me in good stead with businesses I later created.

Today, Jason runs a company he founded called Schmick Scratch & Dent Assist, which employs over sixty people and is worth roughly $40 million.

In 2003 Jason sold his Jim's region; he had been with Jim's for over twelve years and was looking for a new challenge. Six months later the idea of running Jim's in the UK struck. Jim was happy for him to try, and Jason went on a reconnaissance mission. He decided it was a good opportunity, so he took on the rights for Jim's Mowing in the UK in 2004. Jason said,

> Jim wanted me to take over everything in the Mowing division, so I cut a deal with [the existing shareholder] which meant he was a 30 per cent shareholder in the UK rights assuming he stuck around for a period of time.

Jason and his wife, Justine, and twin three-year-old boys moved there, set up a house and office and started selling franchises.

> We did it on a stringent budget, which is what Jim says is always the best way. In the beginning things were slow. I didn't make much. Nobody knew about Jim's Mowing in the UK.

With time and hard work Jason built Jim's Mowing in the UK, reaching ten franchisees by June 2006. Things were good, until the relationship between Jason and the other shareholder soured. Jason had been planning to move back to Australia anyway to be closer to family, so he sold his share to Paul Carr in 2006. Paul Carr and the other shareholder became partners, with Paul putting in a lot of his own money to help continue the growth of Jim's Mowing in the UK over the next couple of years. 'He put a couple of hundred thousand pounds in I imagine,' Jason said. In 2009 Jim's relationship with Paul Carr was to sour badly, with disastrous results discussed in chapter 14.

Today, Jim's Mowing in the UK only has sixteen franchisees, three franchisee–franchisors, and three full-time franchisors. It still hasn't taken off like many hoped.

Jim's call centre

In 2003 Jim advertised for a call centre manager, and Jill Stallworthy applied. She had been working in the corporate world, managing a call centre with 120 staff, but she was sick of the long hours — she wanted more time with her children. She went to her interview in a corporate suit and was greeted by a big huntsman on the wall of the meeting room. 'I was totally overdressed — I thought I was in hillbilly land!' Jill laughed. 'But then I realised people here are down to earth and I could be myself.' She was offered the job and, despite it only paying her $45 000 (a significant decrease from her previous wage of $120 000), she accepted. 'I wanted the lifestyle change,' Jill said. 'And I've been so blessed. You know how they say there's a defining moment in your life? Coming here was mine.'

Jill began just before Christmas 2003. The Melbourne call centre only took calls from Melbourne and parts of regional Victoria, and the team was small. She was used to KPIs, processes for feedback and monitoring, one-on-ones with staff, and internal communication, but 'there was no adherence to anything,' Jill said. She quickly put it all into place.

As well as the Melbourne call centre, there were other Jim's call centres around the country run by franchisors. However in Jill's eyes the franchisors managing them were 'probably not objective, so processing complaints, for example, may not have been done properly, because you don't want to put in a complaint against your own franchisee'. Jill organised conference calls with the other call centres and helped them implement processes to run more smoothly. 'I think they resented it but I actually didn't care, because I could see they weren't giving the right service,' Jill said. She worked to unify the scattered call centres to run like a team.

Back then the call centres closed early in the evenings, and from midday Saturday to Monday morning. Today they are open seven days a week. 'Customers' expectations are very different today,' Jill said.

In 2005 Jim told Jill he was considering selling the call centre because it was costing more money than it was making, which wasn't sustainable. Every franchisor paid Jim a fee per franchisee per month for the running costs, which came out of the fees the franchisees paid their franchisors, to ensure the call centre wouldn't have to move overseas.

Jill went away to look at the budget and profit and loss statements, reviewing all the expenses, and realised that 'things just weren't adding up,' she said. She told Jim, 'There are hire purchases for boats, cars and leases for things. Are these yours?' They weren't. 'He realised that some people working in National Office were actually cheating him,' Jill said. She calculated the call centre would indeed be sustainable without the call centre's funds being used on personal expenses. Jim was thrilled to learn the call centre wouldn't need to be sold.

Just before Christmas 2005 Jim asked Jill if she would like to lease the call centre from him, meaning she would receive a percentage of the income collected. After reviewing the financials Jill asked her twenty-two-year-old daughter, Rebecca, if she would like to do it together. Rebecca had worked at National Office before and had complementary skills to her mum, 'So we went into business together;

it was really lovely,' Jill said. Rebecca and Jill still manage the Jim's call centre today.

Up in flames

In 2006 the call centre faced a challenge. There is a little cottage on the 20-acre property that Rebecca was renting with her boyfriend. At 10.30 pm on 9 October Rebecca heard her dogs barking, which was odd. One barked at everything, but the other only barked if something was amiss. 'Maybe it's a possum,' she thought, and then their lights flickered. Her boyfriend looked outside 'and he saw this massive wall of flames' where the call centre was, Jill said. 'Rebecca rang me screaming, "The place is on fire!"'

Jill raced over and found the road had been blocked off by the fire brigade. 'My daughter's in there, and my business,' she told them, and they let her through. The call centre building was on fire, along with some trees next to it. 'I was wearing my bloody slippers, I don't know what I was thinking because of course there was water everywhere!' Jill recalled.

Jim, who lived next door, had been first to arrive, followed by the fire brigade. 'It was chaos, with fire trucks everywhere and flames bursting out of the building,' Jim said.

Three people were especially nervous while the flames demolished the call centre. One was Jill. 'I kept thinking, "I hope I turned that coffee urn off, I swear to God I hope I turned it off, I was the last to leave,"' Jill recalled. 'And this horrible feeling goes over you — imagine if you caused a fire?' The other was the Test and Tag franchisee who had been checking the safety of all the plugs and computer monitors in the call centre that very day. He hadn't checked the last two computers because the girls needed them to take calls, 'so he was going to come back the next day to do them,' Jim said, 'and that night the place burned down. I tell you what, he was sweating blood. What if the fire was caused by something he'd missed?' Jim was also nervous, because he didn't really need the building that was burning, and he didn't want to be accused of arson.

The next morning showed the damage: the whole call centre had burned down, along with the adjoining dining room, training room, another big room, meeting room and toilets. 'You couldn't even tell there was a toilet bowl or a tap; there was no evidence of the toilet block, the ferocity of it was just incredible.' The auditorium was attached to the call centre by a walkway, which had burned down, but the fire brigade had arrived in time to save the auditorium.

The fire brigade brought in a cherry picker and managed to pull out the coffee urn and some fluorescent lights to investigate how the fire had started. From a hotspot on the ceiling they concluded that an old computer monitor was the culprit — one of the two the franchisee had not been able to check. Jill, the franchisee and Jim were all very relieved.

The space is now a concrete area where surplus trailers are stored. 'It makes a good advert for the Test and Tag division,' Jim said. 'This is what can happen if you don't use our services!'

The call centre had to keep answering calls, so Jill organised for them to be diverted to the Adelaide call centre, which was the next biggest. Some staff flew over there to help.

Rebecca and Jill immediately focused on setting up a new call centre. Luckily there was an unused building on the property, but it hadn't been renovated yet and 'was just putrid,' Jill said. They had it pest-controlled and cleaned, carpet was laid, office furniture delivered and Optus installed a new phone software system. Ten working days after the fire, the new Melbourne call centre was operational. 'We were pretty proud,' Jill said. The call centre is still run out of this building today.

Consolidating the call centres

Over the following few years Jim bought the other call centres, except the one in New South Wales, which he just took back at the end of a contract period. Peter Hansen, the owner for New South Wales, is understandably very annoyed that everyone else got paid decent money for their call centres, and he didn't. He was left with the shell of a call centre: the office space, desks, phones, computers and other equipment.

Jim said, 'Maybe I should have paid him for it too, but the contract had ended and I was in my rights to take it back and run it from Melbourne. Plus I'd just made him a very good deal, allowing him to buy out his partner without paying any commission'.

Jill said, 'There was a lot of resistance' to the consolidation of the call centres, as many franchisors and franchisees knew the names of staff in the call centre in their state, and liked it that way. Jim, wanting to ensure consistency, went ahead anyway, and the franchisors and franchisees soon realised the voices on the other end of the phone were just as friendly and helpful in Melbourne.

The New Zealand call centres were the last to be brought to Melbourne, in April 2018. Today the Jim's call centre has over forty staff. They take calls for Australia, New Zealand and British Columbia (Canada).

Jim showed me how quickly calls are answered in the call centre. We watched a screen showing the incoming calls, which flash blue when answered. Of the ten calls we watched, most were answered in three seconds, with only one taking ten seconds. 'We try to have a very limited wait-time,' Jill told us. The call centre is purposely overstaffed to make this possible, and it helps that the calls are usually quick. 'People usually just ask for a service, and you take their details and find the right person for them,' Jill said. 'But in the middle of spring on a Monday morning, there is a queue.' Every call is recorded. The call centre also does web chatting with franchise prospects on the Jim's Group website, and some of the divisional websites.

When asked about her experience of Jim, Jill responded, 'At first I thought he would be hard to talk to, but I was just me and I talked'. They quickly grew to have mutual respect.

We have a strong relationship, I've learned lots from him. All I've ever done is everything I can for Jim, I have enormous respect for him. I love his drive for customer service, never being satisfied. It drives and inspires other people. He has very high expectations, but not unreasonable nor about something he wouldn't do himself. He knows his weaknesses and strengths. He knows he's not a social person, so he surrounds himself with a good team.

At training Mike Davenport makes the point to potential new franchisees:

Our call centre does a fantastic job. The one thing you don't do is abuse them. They take a lot of calls, and probably will make the odd mistake, but they're great people. I encourage everyone to go down sometime during training, put on some headphones and listen in.

He explained that 99 per cent of calls are answered in one minute, and that sometimes the staff have to deal with some interesting conversations. 'Once a customer called and said, "Hi, I want to get my dog washed". "Certainly, sir. Where do you live?" "Not telling you".'

Constant change

Jim is known to change his mind often, coming up with new ideas of things to do and how things can be done. Shirley Harry, who worked for Jim for twenty years, said,

> he changes his mind *a lot* a lot. He'd come up with a new concept and say, 'I want this done straight away put it in the contracts,' and maybe a week or month later say, 'Nah, it doesn't work'.

The minutes from a 2009 meeting of the advisory committee show that point 19 was

> Minimising of Contract alterations. Since Aug 2006 (Ver7) to Oct 2009 (Ver 34) we have had 27 updates and modifications. Let's limit this to 1 update every 6 months. Also a log of changes must be maintained.

Shirley Harry remembered this time well: 'People were getting really frustrated'.

Jason Jaap, the franchisee then franchisor who grew Jim's in the UK, said that in the early days Jim 'changed his mind all the time. He can be very stubborn and erratic'. Brendan Hill observed that 'in some sense he's very flexible when changing his views and ways of doing things, but the fundamental character of Jim doesn't change at all'.

Leah Cadwallader, an employee since May 2013, explained that when drafting new contracts they'll ask Jim what he wants, draft it,

> and of course in the time it takes us to draft a contract from scratch he changes his mind twenty times, or wants to put extra things in, or wants to take things out based on feedback.

Leah laughed. 'So drafting can take us quite a while.' She was warned by her colleagues when she started,

> and I just keep warning everyone else who starts here: if you have a task that is going to take a few days to do, be aware it's going to change in that time.

Staff often find that something they've worked on for days is no longer necessary. They shared they can see the positives of this for the business, but it can be tiring. Jim's flexibility can drive great change, or upset the apple cart.

'There are many, many things I've worked on which ended up either not succeeding or not going anywhere. It was frustrating,' Brendan Hill said.

> If there is anybody in this world who is not subject to the sunk-cost fallacy, it would be Jim. He's the exact opposite. Jim always looks forward, looking at what new opportunity is currently on the table, and is ruthlessly pragmatic in what he's choosing to do next. You may disagree with his attitude, with how and why he's doing things, with his management style, et cetera, but at the end of the day he has built the largest franchise group in the country.

11

Jim's Training

Jim's Training is very unique, in that prospects attend it *before* signing a franchise agreement. As Mike Davenport, the current training manager, explained,

> Most franchises say, 'Great that you want to purchase. Pay me and then do our training course'. But we flip it on its head. We say, 'Come and do the course first and then sign the agreement if you wish to go ahead'. So there's a lot of pressure on presenters to do a great job.

It is a part of Jim's transparent sales process that began when he first started his franchise. Today at training, attendees receive a thick, heavy manual with everything they need to know about running a home-service business, plus they are walked through every aspect of the business by professional, engaging presenters. Attendees only sign to join Jim's after being taught everything they need to know, 'so they can take our manuals and go set up their own business', Mike said.

Silvia Valeri, a staff member since June 2009, shared a similar sentiment.

> The Jim's Group is very open. Part of my job is having people in and discussing how Jim's works, how we franchise, how we bring regions on, how we bring divisions on, how we bring franchisees on, et cetera. We are very happy to share. If you can go replicate what we have done, go for it. We've been around for twenty-nine years.

Training's early days

In the beginning there was no formal training at all, just a few days in the field with a successful franchisee. Later, Jim set up a course in Melbourne with Joe Kerlin, a local franchisor, but it wasn't extensive enough. Mike Davenport recalled those days.

> In the early 2000s the training only went for two to three days and was run out of a scout hall opposite the Bayswater office. I don't think it had heating, and we would go to a local pie shop for lunch.

Benn Ward recalled that

> Back then there was not a great deal of training, no mention of safety. We were sent our jobs on a pager, and would duck to a phone box to ring the client.

Back then the Melbourne training was only for Victorian franchisees, with training also done in satellite centres across Australia, New Zealand, Canada and the UK (though some locations and divisions had no training at all). There was no way Jim could make sure the quality of each training was consistent, and he wasn't satisfied with the training run from Melbourne either.

In late 2006, to fix these issues, Jim proposed that all new Australian and New Zealand franchisees fly to Melbourne for a comprehensive two-week course. This caused an uproar, with franchisors telling Jim he was preventing them from running their business because the extra cost would hurt franchise sales. The franchisors running the local courses were also unhappy. But Jim thought it was the best solution because he attributed the rapid growth and success of the Fencing and Test and Tag divisions to their heavy investment in training. Plus, he said that franchisees from Tasmania and the ACT already flew to Melbourne for training, 'and it did not seem an obstacle for them'.

A compromise was reached. The proposed course was set to five days (later six). To make travelling to Melbourne less of a barrier, National Office subsidised prospective interstate franchisees to compensate for their flight costs. For a time Jim even had UK prospects fly to Melbourne for training. The New Zealanders wanted to run their own training, because of issues with visas for new arrivals in the country. After a trial showed New Zealand's training had good feedback and an attrition rate similar to Australia, they were given permission to continue running training in Auckland, based on the Melbourne format.

In late 2006 Mike Davenport was working at National Office when Greg Puzzolo offered him his role as Mowing Divisional Manager, so he could become CEO, which Mike gladly accepted. Jim told them to employ someone as National Training Manager as part of the plan to improve Melbourne's training.

At the same time Benn Ward, a franchisor-franchisee who had started as a Mowing franchisee ten years before at just eighteen, had back surgery and couldn't mow lawns. Benn saw the training manager job ad, applied and 'was lucky enough to get it,' Benn said.

As part of Mike's role he worked with Benn to improve training, and they became close mates. They designed a thorough program for the course, brought in other trainers and organised the catering. (Back then the catering was done off-site and delivered, whereas today the Foothills Conference Centre provides accommodation and meals.) Before their first training they were both at the venue until 11.30 pm making sure they had all the plastic knives, forks and bowls needed to feed everybody. 'Benn used to do dishes before he went and delivered a session,' Mike recalled.

'Jim used to work us pretty hard [at training]. We'd go till late because he wanted to cram in as much as possible,' Benn said.

> Jim led sessions himself until 9.30 pm, which itself is amazing, and then he would drive the trainees back to their hotel in Lilydale in his old bus. The trainees loved it. The biggest drawcard for the training was the contact they would have with Jim.

One point Jim persistently bugged Benn about was the leftover food. Jim wanted no money wasted so the course could be the lowest possible price, 'but it's hard to not over-order when you're catering for sixty people,' Benn said. I asked Benn how Jim communicated this frustration. Benn said,

> He drives high standards, but he does it with the least amount of words. He would collect feedback on everything from the food to the cleanliness of the rooms to the presenters, and the minute he saw something not good enough, say the food was too unhealthy, he would walk in and say, 'Right, we need to do something about this'. It wasn't that we were having verbal clashes, it was just that I felt the pressure…

One day Benn was driving Jim's bus and a water bottle fell and rolled under the brake pedal and he ran into the back of a car.

'I remember stressing out, wondering how I was going to tell Jim,' Benn said. He told Jim exactly what had happened, and Jim responded calmly: 'You can do it once, but don't do it again'. Benn was surprised at Jim's response. 'He was fine — you just never know what you're going to get with Jim.' Jim self-insures his vehicles, so he had to pay it out personally. 'Overall insurance is a losing proposition,' Jim explained, 'Anything that I can afford to self-insure, I do. And staff tend to be extra careful when they know I'm paying for the damage.'

Fine-tuning training

Mike had been Mowing Divisional Manager for a few months when Jim took him outside and said, 'Look, I don't think you need to come back tomorrow'.

Mike was upset. They 'shared some views pretty quickly, very loudly,' Mike recalled with a wry grin. 'I was pretty disappointed to have lost the role...'

That day he packed up his desk and went home.

In hindsight I never should have had it. I wasn't really right for the role. Jim worked that out quicker than I did; it wasn't a bad decision to let me go.

Mike went home and refocused on being a franchisor-franchisee.

In 2009 Jim rang Mike out of the blue. 'Can you come out and see me?'

Mike drove out, and they sat in the conference centre and Jim said, 'I'd like you to take over the training'.

'Are you kidding me? You know Benn Ward is my best mate at Jim's. You're asking me to take his job!'

'Benn won't have the job next week, I'm getting rid of him.'

'You need to take this to Advisory,' Mike protested.

'I'll take it to Advisory but it's not their decision, it's mine, it's my company,' Jim replied.

Jim's comment about this was,

I know it was harsh, and Benn is a good guy. But as a trainer and organiser, Mike is simply the best. You have to remember that the future of thousands of families depends on how well we do training and no-one is more important than that. Not Benn and not Mike and not me. We all serve the franchisees, and they're our number one priority. I'm just in awe of how smoothly Mike runs things and how good he is in front of a crowd. How does he remember all those people, when there can be up to a hundred and more? And yet in the Mowing divisional role he wasn't that good. Sometimes people have their perfect niche and you just have to find it.

Meanwhile, Mike was flabbergasted and felt awful. 'Jim pretty much pitted me against Benny,' Mike said. 'I don't know how Jim does that sort of stuff, but he does it.' On his drive home Mike called Benn.

'Mate, um, I've been offered a job today.'

'That's great news!' Benn said.

'Well, it depends how you look at it, Benn.'

'Why's that, mate?'

'Well…Jim offered me the National Training Manager role.'

There was silence. Then Benn replied, 'Oh, right'.

Mike said, 'Listen, I've told him he needs to take it to Advisory. I hate to tell you this, but he said he's going to get rid of you next week'.

They talked it through and then Mike said,

I think we've got two options: one is I say no, you lose the job and we lose our training; someone else will come in, we'll lose it and so be it, we're done and dusted and we'll probably never work in National Office again. Or, I take the job and we run it together. Yes, I'll be the figurehead but I'll still be looking for your input.

Benn Ward, to his credit, accepted this. It was discussed at the advisory meeting on 13 November 2009, the minutes of the meeting simply stating:

Jim advised that Mike Davenport would better suit the Training Manager's role as he has proved to be an exceptional trainer and has good ideas to improve training. Mike has accepted the role in consultation with Benn Ward. Mike will be providing Jim with feedback as to how courses can be improved further so that more trainers rate 'excellent' rather than 'good'.

Today Benn still delivers one day of training, 'which shows the type of person he is,' Mike said. They are still best mates.

In jest, right after Mike introduces Benn at training, Benn loves to tell the story of how Mike 'knifed him', calling Mike 'Julia Gillard' because it happened around the time that Julia Gillard took over from Kevin Rudd as prime minister. 'It is quite funny, really, but to straighten the story out, it wasn't exactly me, it was Jim,' Mike said in our interview.

To this day I still don't know why Jim wanted the change. Maybe he saw things that I didn't see, but it was … it was honestly a tough time. But we look back now and have a good laugh.

One night after a training dinner Jim stayed back to sit in on a game Mike and Benn played with the attendees. Mike left the room and Benn told everyone, 'We need to pick a famous person, and we'll see whether Mike can guess it'. Mike came back in, having no idea who they had chosen. However, Mike and Benn had a communication trick that would tell Mike, subtly, the name of the famous person.

They played it a few times, with Jim observing. Each time Mike would guess correctly who they had chosen, but no-one could figure out how Mike was doing it. Again Mike left the room, and this time they chose Ricky Ponting, who was the captain of the Australian Men's Cricket Team at the time.

Once Mike was back in the room Benn said, 'Right we'll get started,' and he clapped three times. 'Come on Mike, guess.' He paused. 'Know what it is? You may be close.' He paused again. 'People struggle with this game.' And he clapped four times. 'Now can you guess it Mike? Try.' And he clapped three times. 'Now can you guess? Go on.'

All of a sudden Jim said, 'Oh, I've got the answer, I know how you're doing it'.

Mike and Benn looked at him. No-one had cracked the code before.

'But who is Ricky Ponting?' Jim asked.

Mike and Benn were dumbfounded. 'He was smart enough to work out what we were doing, but then didn't know who Ricky Ponting was. Classic!' Benn said.

Mike recalled the moment with the same disbelief and amazement.

Jim's not into sport, but it didn't matter he didn't know Ricky Ponting, he still cracked the code ... that's his mind. So we couldn't

play the game with Jim anymore because he used to beat us! It was quite funny. I'll never forget that night he cracked the code.

Training today

The training today is still very similar to what Benn and Mike originally created. It takes up to six days (depending on the division). The first three are generic, and the rest division-specific. One difference is the venue: it's now held at the Foothills Conference Centre. Set among eucalyptus trees, it is a lovely environment for potential franchisees and franchisors to bond at training. Jim offers existing franchisors free meals and low-cost accommodation to encourage them to come to training also, where they can connect with their prospects and build relationships with National Office staff and each other.

On the first day I attended training, I watched Mike seamlessly build rapport with the large group. After asking the group what their reasons for joining Jim's were, he shared that most franchisees 'took a left turn into a totally new career' when they joined Jim's.

At 8.28 am Mike looked at his watch and said, 'Jim will walk through that door at 8.30 am on the dot,' and exactly two minutes later Jim walked in. At every training Jim gives a two-hour session on his ethos, where he talks passionately about customer service.

Jim's customer service ethos

Though Jim can be awkward one-on-one, in front of a crowd he is captivating. He discussed exactly how the most successful franchisees conduct themselves in business, from returning all phone calls within two hours ('How long does it take to make a call today or in two days' time? The same amount! The things that you do to service a client do not take extra time.') and texting immediately if the client doesn't answer the phone, to always wearing their uniform, always going above and beyond to totally satisfy the customer and always arriving when they say they will. Jim advised that in home-service businesses it can be hard to predict exactly how long jobs will take,

> so don't say 'I'll be there at 10 am', it's too hard. Say 'I'll be there between 9 am and 11 am'. And if you're running late call, and if they don't answer, text.

Jim also shared stories from when he was mowing lawns himself, delighting the audience with the story of how he bought one of Australia's first whipper snippers. But he always returned to the importance of great customer service.

> You have to satisfy the client. Once we had a customer who wanted a tree taken down from the front of their house. Now this franchisee did an absolutely superb job! What do you think the problem was?

Here he paused for effect.

> It was the wrong tree! I just kept asking the customer 'What can I do to make it right?' It's not a matter of how technically perfect a job is done, it's about *customer satisfaction*.

A little later Jim said,

> now, if you do not give a clear, written quote to the client, and there is any disagreement between you and the client about exactly what the job entailed — and believe me this is common — you will do whatever the customer says. It's not a matter of who is right or wrong, you may be completely right. But when this comes back to the franchisors and me you will have to do whatever the customer

says. And if you don't do it, somebody else will and you will be billed for it. It's as harsh as that. And it's not because we don't believe you, it's because you are professionals and know you need to give written, clear quotes.

Jim warned them that he will usually take the client's side, even if it seems unfair, because the most important thing is that clients receive excellent service and walk away from the experience pleased.

Jim is big on evidence — if a client answers the customer satisfaction survey saying that the franchisee didn't call back within two hours, it is automatically lodged into the system as a complaint, even if the client didn't actually complain about it. Jim will only delete the complaint if the franchisee sends screenshots showing they called the client within two hours and also sent a text if they couldn't get through.

'We monitor complaints very carefully,' Jim said. 'It doesn't always mean the complaint is fair. Sometimes the client is really unfair.'

When Jim shared the strict nature of the complaint system it was an inspiring speech. The prospective franchisees walked away with a clear understanding of just how passionate Jim is about customer service, and commented on how inspired they felt.

In the following session Mike asked the group, 'What's good about feedback?'

'You can see where you need to improve.'

'You can learn.'

'Constructive criticism.'

'Yeah,' Mike paused. 'When you get your first complaint I want to hear you say "constructive criticism",' which got a laugh. But he is right — Jim's complaint system seems very uninspiring and unfair when franchisees experience it themselves.

Constant feedback

At the end of Jim's session he put his email and mobile number on the board.

> You have a direct line to me. If you have a problem, the first person to speak to is your franchisor, but if your franchisor can't answer it, or your problem is with your franchisor, or if you can't reach your franchisor for some reason, contact me. I want you to write [my contact details] down. Any franchisee can contact me anytime you like. I want you to contact me.
>
> In actual fact one of my biggest issues is that franchisees don't contact me because they don't want to bother me, but I am remarkably easy to get in contact with. I don't do an awful lot — I've got great people who run the business. Being in touch with franchisees, dealing with customer complaints and dealing with franchisee issues is my major job. You are everything. You are vitally important. You are our major focus. Please don't think I'm too busy.

After stating his intention to 'talk to every single one' of the attendees over the next few days, Jim walked off stage.

Mike has been presenting for a long time and is very good at it, but there has been a lot of changeover in presenters over the years. 'Jim sets a high standard and ... some people fall out quite quickly,' Mike told me. 'Standing in front of a group of people isn't always the easiest thing to do, especially the first time.' The presenters aren't rated every few months, or annually — they are rated after every single training.

Jim has a policy that new presenters get three chances for poor ratings, after which if they don't improve they're fired. Mike said,

All of our attendees get a sheet of paper after every single session with four options: excellent, very good, adequate and poor. Jim sets a target of being 75 per cent 'excellent'.

Every Monday morning after a training week Jim sends Mike an email with a spreadsheet showing the collated feedback. Mike said,

Sometimes I won't open the email because I'm thinking, 'What is the feedback going to be like?' Jim laughs about it; he seems to think it's a great joke. I don't.

Jim uses the feedback to assess how every presenter did, and decide whether someone is doing well, needs to improve or needs to go. 'We've had a few comings and goings along the way,' Mike said. 'But it's great because it's an important course people pay to come to, we need to deliver damn well and I have no problems with that.'

Jim commented that he himself gets rated, along with everyone else:

Mike and others often rate better than me. If I get a poor response one week I want to work out what went wrong and how I can improve. There's nothing like constant feedback to keep you on your toes.

Jim is very proud of the training course.

Before starting it we used to lose 17 per cent of our franchisees in the first year, which was consistent across the years and in the different states and countries. Now it's around ten per cent. People may have grizzled about the change, but hundreds of people have succeeded as franchisees where previously they would have failed. That's what matters to me.

A different side of Jim

On the Thursday evening of training week there is a dinner for the new franchisors, which Jim always goes to. Mike said of Jim,

> You see such a different side to Jim that you've never seen before and you'll never see again. He's got the best party tricks around. Jim's not a comedian, but when he's got control of the night you've got people around the room laughing, Jim's having a laugh, it's a great night. It's just remarkable.

Haydar Hussein, the divisional of Jim's Cleaning, said at the franchisor dinner 'he is the life of the party, which is very interesting,' given Jim is normally not that way inclined. 'He does little acts and tells us little stories; he doesn't talk about personal experiences; it's just riddles and stuff like that,' Haydar explained.

Craig Pritchard, an employee, said,

> It's like a switch is flicked and Jim becomes this performer; you won't get it until you see it. It's completely different to what I expected, even though I was told about it beforehand. He sort of changes and becomes the centre of attention, which he says he doesn't really like. It's good to see Jim in a different light from day to day.

Needless to say, I was very intrigued when I attended a franchisor dinner. I witnessed Jim moving from table to table, chatting with the prospective franchisors. After we'd eaten and the plates were cleared it began with Tino Grossi, CEO at the time, saying, 'Jim, tell us that riddle!' Jim grinned, looking slightly awkward, but as soon as he began the awkwardness disappeared and he was incredibly entertaining.

Everyone tried guessing the riddle's answer, and he was delighted when they guessed wrong. 'He revels in the fact that people can't get the answer,' Mike told me. After that there was another riddle, called 'The White Hats'. Numerous long-time franchisors told me that they still don't get 'that bloody riddle', so it was remarkable when someone on the night cracked it in less than ten minutes — Jim was impressed.

Next came 'the knife game', in which Jim arranges a handful of knives in a certain pattern, and tells everyone to guess the number it represents. Most have no idea and guess wrong, so he rearranges the knives, and asks 'What number is it now?' Slowly people catch on with how the trick works, roaring with laughter at the remaining few still guessing wrongly. 'He does that knife show pretty much every single time,' Haydar Hussein sighed and grinned, having witnessed it one too many times.

'I know those jokes and riddles by heart, but it's always entertaining,' Paul Commerford, the divisional for Building Inspections, said. For the new franchisors in the room, the evening is a hoot.

In a later interview Jim shared that he struggles in large groups where it's too noisy, and I expressed surprise, bringing up the franchisor dinner. Jim replied,

> **My way of coping with my poor social skills is I do a certain kind of act. I'm not naturally a party-type person. I can do that kind of stuff, but it's learned.**

I pointed out that some of his jokes were entirely spontaneous, playing off a joke Tino had said, and he seemed surprised with himself. Though Jim's humour doesn't come out often, he does have a quick, intelligent wit. Craig Parke mentioned, 'In the beginning he couldn't speak to crowds, but he got better and better'.

Jim and HIS UNIFORM

Jim is known to always wear his Jim's uniform. Initially he wore his green Jim's Mowing top, the same one Mowing franchisees wear, no matter the occasion. Andrew Parke recalled,

> Jim has no problem, and he has done so many times, turning up to a meeting, for example with someone senior at NAB or something like that, in his dirty old work boots and his green uniform.

At a certain point, with many other divisions launching, someone suggested that Jim should perhaps wear a 'Jim's Group' shirt instead of the Mowing top. And he has, every day since. Along with the same pants, boots and jacket. As Cynthia Tjong, head of finance at the Jim's Group, commented with amazement,

> Every day he always wears the same thing. It's the same uniform shirt with the logo and black shoes. Every day, for years. Even at home. I have never seen him wearing anything different.

Prathamesh Bhoir, the former head chef at Foothills, only ever saw Jim wear something else once.

> He had a small function for Jim's Mum's Week, a small high tea, and I've never seen Jim so jovial. He was not Jim. And he was dressed differently! Otherwise Jim always wears his Jim's Group shirt, his boots, his black pants. I have seen him for eight years like that, regardless of big meeting, small meeting, national conference.

Sure enough, at the 2018 national conference gala dinner, among a sea of suits and beautiful dresses, Jim wore his Jim's attire. Someone jokingly asked him why, suggesting he wear something else to the gala dinner. 'This is my brand, I always represent my brand,' Jim said, before admitting, 'and I hate suits and ties'. As his sixteen-year-old daughter Sylvia said, 'Dad does not care what anybody thinks of him, he's not self-conscious at all. He would like literally go out wearing a garbage bag — but Mum wouldn't let him'.

Craig Parke recalled that the only time he saw Jim in a suit was at the funeral of Andrew Parke's daughter.

It was very good of him; he came to the funeral and he wore a suit. It only takes little things sometimes. That was 2004 and even now I'm saying it was a good thing. The small things can go a long way.

12

The Franchisee Experience

Jim's franchisees all have different stories of how they came to buy a franchise, but there are many similar themes. For many, they wanted to work for themselves and have flexibility in when and where they worked. Others were retrenched and didn't know what to do next. Others simply wanted a change: something that would replace their income where they didn't have to sit in an office all day.

Jyosh Polea-Vizcarra wanted to spend more time with her kids. 'It's been really good. As soon as you join there's a system you follow,' Jyosh said. 'I love helping people, so Jim's is a great thing to do. After twelve months my husband actually left his job and joined me.'

Meg Leaney was a chef, who after running her own business for twenty-one years needed a change of profession and lifestyle. 'I'd been googling about becoming a dog groomer, and a Jim's advertisement came up for "Franchisees wanted in Canberra", so I made enquiries,' Meg said. She looked at other dog grooming franchises, but

Jim's was the fairest on franchise fees, and the most professional. If you had said to me a year ago, 'You'll be a franchisee this time next year', I would have laughed! But there was genuinely something about Jim's.

Joe Badr, in Canada, wanted to get out of the office.

A lot of franchises take percentages of income: the bigger you get, the more you have to pay. But with Jim's it's that one flat fee. I had three trailers running and was still paying that one fee. I like that I can expand my business without being charged more.

In 2014 Sharon Connell wanted a business that would replace her income. Her job was so stressful she 'used to vomit in the carpark before work,' Sharon said. She worked long hours, her husband worked permanent night shifts and they wanted a change. She looked at all sorts of businesses before coming across Jim's Cleaning. 'I didn't like it because I didn't want to be a cleaner,' Sharon said. But the franchisor gave her Jim's book *Selling by Not Selling*, and her husband read it and insisted Sharon read it too. 'The minute I finished reading I emailed the franchisor, "Okay, I'm in",' Sharon said. 'I wanted to be in business and help people, and with Jim's you can do that and make a good income. I just love what Jim's stands for.'

Sharon began as a Cleaning franchisee, then a Cleaning franchisor, and then became the divisional of Dog Wash. She said,

We don't have to worry about paying the bills, which is a fantastic place to be. My husband quit his job and works full time for me now, and he gets to do the things he loves; he bought shares in an aeroplane and goes flying.

One of Sharon's franchisees, a single mum, called one day 'laughing her head off' because her water heater had broken. 'That's not good…' Sharon replied, confused.

'Yes it is, because I paid cash to fix it!' The franchisee exclaimed, explaining,

> Before joining Jim's the kids and I would have had to go to Mum's every night for a shower, and I would have had to borrow money or get a credit card to fix it. Now I paid cash!

A selective process

While becoming a franchisee can change a person's life, not everyone is suited to it. The selection process is thorough. Jim gives a talk at every franchisor training on the importance of franchisors being selective. He asks them to look for people who give good customer service, who ask good questions, are dressed professionally, have a stable and supportive family, have a job background showing initiative and responsibility and have a community service activity. 'And make sure they are someone you feel comfortable with and like, because it's a long relationship,' Jim said. One of his common mantras is 'when in doubt, say no'. It was one of the aspects he most appreciated about the way Test and Tag was run.

Many franchisors explained that they are selective in who they sell franchises to. Of the Mowing division, Anthony Silverman said, 'The selection process is all about attitude, what people are like: Are they friendly, good with people? We teach the rest'.

A few franchisors commented that others were too slack. Franchises were being sold to people who couldn't speak English well enough to quote well, and thus build a successful business. Others argued franchisors could be too selective and not give people who are new to Australia a chance. Just because a person 'is not fluent and he can't do the Aussie accent' doesn't mean they don't deserve the opportunity. They 'will benefit from it, and that is what motivates me,' one person said.

While they disagreed about criteria, both sides were equally committed to finding good franchisees for whom Jim's would be a great opportunity.

Said Haydar Hussein, the divisional of Cleaning,

What I love — and I haven't been able to get a bank to understand this yet — is that a high percentage of Jim's Cleaning franchisees will join us with nothing, scrape up their $20 000 to come in, and within twelve months they will be buying a house. They come from a war-torn country and they have the hunger of ownership; they want a house.

Peter Hansen spoke of the cultural differences in his region. 'I've got Africans, Anglos, Vietnamese, Chinese, Indians, Afghans, I even had a Mongolian at one stage.' While the first impediment is having the money to buy a franchise, 'the second biggest impediment for refugees coming here, that causes them to struggle, is a lack of English,' Peter said.

But beyond that, if they can string some words together it's easy to get by. I have a Nepalese guy, a lovely bloke, who's an accountant by profession but he's a Jim's Mowing guy here. He said 'Peter! Peter! I don't ever want to leave this business because I'm making so much money, so much money, I can't believe it!' To me that is job satisfaction.

In 2015 Harley McKean was in his early twenties and was running his own business, but he had some cash flow problems. Harley said,

> I thought about buying a mowing franchise, but the franchisor said, 'Financially it's probably not the right time for you. Come back to us in a couple more years when you're a bit more experienced and you'll be kicking goals'. And I really respected that. Even at the time I thought it was cool. As a franchisor you should at some point sell franchises, but it's not like they're just picking anyone. How often do you come across that? And he was right, I probably wasn't mature enough to run a full-time thing.

The franchisor stayed in touch with Harley over the next two years, by which point he was looking at dog-grooming businesses. 'I interviewed basically everyone in Melbourne that offered dog grooming as a franchise,' Harley said. 'But I liked the way Jim's does it.' Harley became a Jim's Dog Wash franchisee in late 2017.

Financially rewarding work

Though Jim's is a rigid system to operate in, with strict policies around customer service and complaints, there is no doubt that most franchisees make good money when they follow the system. Jim explained, 'Most franchisees earn above the average wage in Australia, and they're doing things like pool cleaning, paving and building inspections. We recommend our franchisees charge at least $60 an hour once they get the hang of the job'.

Anthony Silverman said that some of his franchisees

> make $250000 to $300000 revenue a year mowing lawns. It's really big money, with very little responsibility other than to your clients. You just need to pay your franchise fees and do good work. And we sell

the businesses so cheap. People spend $400 000 buying coffee shops, and after they've paid everybody might make $60 000 to $80 000 a year for that investment. When I started I turned over $113 000 in my first year — 1993. I was only working Monday to Friday. I never started before 8 am. I was going to see my kids do their sports. Today I've got guys making $3000 a week, working three to four days a week. There's serious money in this business — people don't believe it. The biggest problem when selling franchises is that people hear this and think 'That can't be true,' but it's really true.

I asked many franchisees if Jim's claim of earning $60 an hour was accurate from their experience. A number said that in some states (e.g. Tasmania), it is hard to earn that much mowing lawns. Others said that some divisions can't charge as much as others. On the flipside, many said, 'Sixty dollars an hour? I earn way more than that!' A husband-and-wife team shared they turn over roughly $200 000 a year with them both working, though of course turnover is different from profit. One franchisee said the only thing keeping him in Jim's is how much he earns.

Sharon Connell, the divisional of Dog Wash, said, 'If you follow the system you'll be successful, you can't help it. It's the most amazing system'. She went on to explain that sometimes a franchisee will 'get a bit lazy' with following Jim's system, and they start doing things differently,

and all of the sudden they're not doing very well. I teach my franchisees to follow the system: call back immediately; quote in person; smile, wave, be friendly; do a great job; ask for referrals.

Glenn Camilleri bought a Jim's Mowing franchise in 1992. 'I was the hundred and twentieth,' Glenn said. Today he runs his company EzyRental, which rents out mowing equipment to Mowing franchisees who can't buy it outright yet. He said that being a successful franchisee 'all comes down to mindset.'

> Some people don't take responsibility. When I trained guys out in the field I'd say, 'Run it like you own the business'. The guys that don't, I reckon they struggle. Because on a day like today [a rainy, cold winter's day] you won't have too many people calling in for gardening work, so you've got to be able to develop business to get that extra work through the seasons.

Katherine Doe, who worked with Jim's in many capacities over the years, commented that

> Franchisees should expect to match their income, and if it's more than that, great. The divisions are different, some are higher priced services than others. Not all franchisees make good money; not all people are cut out to run a business, even with all the support they get at Jim's.

Jim emphasised that Anthony Silverman's numbers do not apply to everyone.

> Anthony was especially good, which is one reason he became a franchisor, but most franchisees probably don't make much more than $100 000 a year. And while we don't ask them for their figures, in the last survey around ten per cent reported poor income. The business works for most, but definitely not for everyone.

The complaint system: Guilty until proven innocent

Jim is perhaps the only owner of a large organisation who personally reads every complaint, every day. He manages the complaint system and is the only person with the power to delete a complaint. When

I asked franchisees what they thought of the complaint system, the general sentiment was that they like it, as it ensures everyone does good work. Franchisee Brett Ardley said, 'It's a necessary evil; it's good for the brand. And I don't get many [complaints] — I probably wouldn't think it was good if I did'. This seems to be a common feeling, as most of the franchisees I interviewed mentioned they hardly receive complaints. Franchisee George Donopolous said, 'The complaint system is good; it keeps everyone on their toes. It makes us do the right thing, giving great service'.

Still, when complaints are received it's upsetting, particularly if they seem unfair. Anthony Silverman acknowledged Jim's passion for customer service,

> But I think he takes it a bit far sometimes. If a customer has an issue with a franchisee he always takes the customer's word for it. If a franchisee has a problem with a franchisor, he takes the franchisee's word for it. He's very structured that way; you're guilty until proven innocent, the opposite of a democratic justice system.

Jim sees most things as black or white, with no grey, 'but in life and business there is lots of grey,' Anthony said. 'Still, it's also a big reason the Jim's franchise is what it is; because of his push to provide great service.'

Jim agreed that he sees a franchisee as guilty until proven innocent,

> because if I delete complaints on the basis of a plausible story then customer service collapses, and so do leads and franchisee income. An individual complaint may be unfair, but a single complaint means nothing. It takes dozens of complaints and poor surveys to breach or terminate a franchisee, and there's no way [franchisees who get lots of complaints] are treated unfairly.

At the training I attended, a UK franchisee in the audience voiced his frustration about Jim always wanting proof before removing a complaint.

'Are you a good operator?' Jim asked.

'Yes,' he replied.

'Do you think that nearly every other franchisee thinks of themselves as a good operator?'

'Hmm, probably.'

Jim replied,

And do you think they all tell the truth, all the time? You tell the truth, and one of the reasons I know you do is because you're a good operator. But the worst franchisees in the system, let me tell you — every time they get a problem it's never their fault. 'The customer did this, the customer did that.' If I were to listen to every franchisee and go through deleting all the complaints based on their word — the system wouldn't work. That's why we can't delete your unfair complaints unless you have evidence, even though we *know* you're a good operator and we *know* it was an unfair complaint.

The complaints we get are *very* unevenly distributed. Most complaints come from less than 10 per cent of our franchisees. The complaint system is not there to look after good-quality franchisees like yourself, because we don't need to. We can see you're good. It's there to keep an eye on the ones who are not doing the right thing. But you're right, it's very upsetting for someone with a great record to see a complaint on the system. But the trouble is, the reason we *know* you're a great franchisee is *because* of the system. Ironically, if we adopted the policy that we'd delete complaints based on what a franchisee says, we wouldn't know how good an operator you are.

'I understand that, now you say it,' the guy replied.

'Understand this: it's a very, very tough system, and sometimes it will hurt you. But it's vital for our success.'

Richard Long, an employee since July 2013, said at first he thought the complaint system was cold.

> Then, thinking about it, it made sense. If there are franchisees not pulling their weight they are hurting the brand. A brand that feeds a lot of families. Imagine if Jim was soft ... a less rigorous complaint system, less franchisees given breaches and terminated, customer service slackens, job quality slips ... less clients. You need that real strong guy at the top.

Soon after being employed Ben Siddons, a divisional manager at National Office, experienced just how passionate Jim is about handling complaints. A customer complained and Ben worked hard to find a resolution, emailing Jim with the amount it would cost to repair the issue. 'I got in massive trouble, it was the first time I copped it from Jim that and I couldn't understand what I'd done wrong,' Ben said. It turned out that what he'd done wrong was handle a complaint. 'Jim wanted to handle the complaint himself! It was the strangest thing for me,' Ben explained, coming from environments where calling the head of the company for them to deal with a complaint would get you fired. 'Jim called the customer himself and got it sorted ... It's incredibly powerful, having *Jim* call the customer to resolve it,' Ben said. He was astonished at Jim's passion. 'Classic Jim: this is the only place you can get fired for getting involved in the complaint system, that's how seriously he takes it.'

Franchisees regularly call Jim asking for a complaint or bad survey to be removed, and he explains that he won't remove it without evidence. They are rarely friendly conversations, but Jim is willing to be the bad cop to uphold the brand, 'because I know that the welfare of thousands of franchisees depends on high standards, which keeps the work flowing in. And this is what I always try to explain to them'. He is happy to remove a complaint when there is clear evidence, and he typically does this 'several times a day'. He said,

> My absolute favourite job is when a franchisee sends me adequate evidence to get an unfair complaint or survey deleted. I do it and congratulate them on their win and if they have a great star rating I congratulate them on that also. It feels really good to say something nice, and promote customer service.
>
> I also really like congratulating a franchisor on a job well done, such as when they've turned a franchisee around by coaching them on how to reduce complaints ... Or when they deal well with a difficult client. The perception is that I always back the client but that's not true. In one case recently we supported a franchisee in court, when a client said they damaged their carpet and the expert evidence showed they did not. We even paid the ridiculous judgement the court gave against him.

Though Jim is known to be tough on complaints, he is not erratic. He has a rigorous complaint system that he always follows, to the letter, no matter how close someone may be with him. He won't give favours. The integrity of the complaint system — and the success of Jim's — always comes first.

13

'A Serial Firer'

Many people I interviewed described National Office as 'a revolving door'; Jim has a reputation for being a serial firer. He will fire quickly if someone is not doing a good job, though he'll often try to find another role for them first. 'I do not fire lightly,' Jim said.

His strategy in hiring is to choose based on character (as best as he can determine), and from there see how they go in the role.

> I look for character, above all. There was a young man, Joel, who began working for me on a casual basis doing basic, unskilled tasks, and he is now one of my senior managers. He is paid more than double what he started on. I hired him and keep him because of the kind of person he is. When I look for employees, I ignore qualifications. Work background and experience matter more. But the absolute key is character.

From day one Jim trusts new employees to an extreme degree, and if they live up to expectations he is delighted. But if it becomes clear they are not performing well, he fires them. From the outside it looks ruthless. Staff joke about his firing habits, but many I spoke to also respect his firing decisions. They explained it's simply part of business to only keep those who do a good job, and a number said they know they'll always have a job while they're doing good work. Though some staff leave or are fired quickly, Jim has a few staff who have been with him for over twenty years, and multiple others near ten. 'You either spend a very short time or a very long time working with Jim,' Brendan Hill, an employee of fourteen years, said.

> If somebody isn't working out, he won't hang onto them. Some people would call it heartless, but the truth is that he's simply being ruthlessly pragmatic in the way he runs his business.

A revolving door

Craig Parke experienced the 'revolving door' as an employee, franchisor and divisional. 'The staff would just come and go, dozens of them,' Craig said.

While Shirley Harry, who worked with Jim for over twenty years, said that Jim was trusting to a fault, others I interviewed shared that Jim won't tolerate staff members taking him for a ride. They described him as having no feeling of loyalty; if he feels someone isn't adding enough value to justify their salary, they're gone. And it doesn't make sense to him to have them hang around for the four week notice period — he usually wants them out of the office the day he's decided they don't add value.

Phil Maunder, a former state franchisor, said,

> To me the biggest negative is that [Jim] doesn't understand loyalty, building relationships. You can be flavour of the month or flavour

of the year and then all of a sudden you're the worst person he's ever met...

One of his key mottos was 'find the best people and try to keep them', and I think he's found a lot of very good people, but he's failed at keeping them.

I asked Richard Long, the employee who wrote to me describing Jim firing a man a week out from his spouse having a baby, about that episode. 'I only heard about it afterwards,' Richard said.

I was working with him on some stuff, he had a baby coming and was about to go on leave, and the next thing I hear he's gone. That's it.

I asked if Richard could reconcile Jim's firing decisions, and he said he could, quite easily. 'Lots and lots of people rely on the brand and the systems to have income,' Richard said, meaning the thousands of franchisees, hundreds of franchisors and numerous divisionals. 'If anyone is slowing the cogs down I'm all for getting rid of them.'

Just before one of our interviews Jim had fired four people, and he said,

It's not nice, I don't like it, but I have to do it because I've got to look at the greater good of everybody else. When I sit down at staff lunch on Friday it's very noticeable — people rarely sit next to me, it's that aura of power and authority. From some points of view having authority is good, but it's easy to abuse, like when I get angry. I feel bad when I do.

In Brendan Hill's fourteen years at National Office he saw many come and go. 'I don't think the firings were the raving and ranting of a mad dictator,' Brendan said, adding,

When somebody was fired it was because Jim had identified they were simply not contributing enough value to the company to justify a salary. I can't speak for every firing, but the ones I can think of on the whole would probably be …

Here he laughed awkwardly, not finishing the sentence. 'I probably lost a few friends by saying that.'

Leah Cadwallader, an employee since May 2013, agreed with Brendan's sentiment.

I've seen a lot of people come and go. Jim is generally, from what I've seen, reasonably fair to staff members who deserve to be here and are still here. There have been occasions where the pressure has built and we might lose a few people in a very short span, but it's usually the people who aren't pulling their weight.

Though Brendan could see sense in Jim's firings, he couldn't always see sense in who Jim hired.

The other half is making the right selection in the first place. I can think of cases where somebody was put into a role and it should have been obvious they weren't suited. So the firing might have been a consequence of a poor hiring decision in the first place.

Brendan gave an example of a young woman who was hired for an admin role because Jim had met her working at a petrol station, and had had a positive experience. From this limited interaction, he offered her a job at National Office. 'And maybe that sort of thing is a result of Jim's experimental tendencies,' Brendan said.

Brendan's own hiring situation was unique. A man called Jonathan Field was working for Jim and he was a family friend of

Brendan's parents. Outside of work Jonathan ran 'Wiz Kid Nights', where young kids and teens learned about programming, coding and how computers worked. Brendan was fourteen and attended a couple, and Jonathan was so impressed with him that he asked Jim if he'd hire Brendan as a trainee. Brendan was being home schooled so it was possible. Jim, happy to experiment, said yes. Brendan became a full-time employee at fifteen, staying for the next thirteen years.

Jim is known to hire fast. 'I've known him to put an ad on Seek at 9 am, interview at 2 pm and the person starts at 8 am the next morning,' Mike Davenport said.

Silvia Valeri, an outgoing personality with an easy laugh who loves to tease Jim, has worked for him since June 2009. She said,

> If you're going to walk the talk, then do it. Don't spin stuff because Jim will see past that. Jim hires people for a reason. And people leave for a reason. That is just business.

When I asked Archie Hood, a divisional manager, about Jim's reputation as a firer, he had a different response.

> Firer? It's not Jim that does it, it's all the managers. He works off feedback. Firer? Nah. It depends which way you want to look at it. You don't fire someone for the sake of firing someone. It's the worst feeling anyone can ever have.

Despite his reputation, Jim is highly conscious of the importance of keeping good staff happy. Apart from the direct commercial benefits, Jim built Foothills in part to look after and motivate staff.

The Friday lunches we give them have proved very popular, and a free on-site health club will be even better. I hate to lose good people, and the more we can do for them the more likely they are to stay.

I interviewed Prathamesh Bhoir, known as Pratt, in his last week as Head Chef of Foothills after working there for eight years. He was very emotional during our interview, explaining how much the place was like his family and how much he loved working there. He was only leaving because of an opportunity to start his own restaurant in Richmond called 3 Idiots. 'Li and Jim have been the best bosses of my career,' Pratt said with emotion. 'Jim called me up and told me, "You are the heart and soul of this place. You shouldn't go". Wiping a tear away, he added, 'I never had a bitter moment with Jim, it's been fantastic'.

Firing family

Over the years Jim has employed most of his children at some point. He made it clear that being his child got them in, but to stay they had to perform. 'All of them have a great work ethic,' Jim said. Andrew's work on Jim's research has been invaluable. Sarah worked in the call centre and also on his research for a time,

> and I would have loved her to continue. James was brilliant in legal and documents, smart and hardworking. I offered him more than double his current salary to continue, but he wanted to make his own way and I respect that. He'll be a partner in his law firm soon. Tom also worked in documents for a time and had everyone's respect as a hard worker who did not rest on the

family name. Richard also worked for a time as a programmer, and David on the grounds. Jasmine and Esther have both done first-class work in the conference centre. None of them have ever disappointed me.

But not all of Jim's family hiring stories are so peaceful. You may have seen on *Today Tonight* in 2012 that Jim fired his sister Gill. Jim's motivation to hire Gill, who had been working in the UK for a number of years, had been to bring her back to Melbourne so she could spend time with their ailing mother, Margaret. Margaret was developing severe dementia in her senior years, and 'it was awful,' Jim said.

> We'd always been close and I appreciated, so much, her love and advice over the years. She was a highly intelligent woman and it was so upsetting seeing her mind failing like that. I saw her weekly at least, but with Gill in the UK and Lynne and Chris [their siblings] not in contact, I was all she had.

Jim hastened to add that he doesn't blame Lynne in any way: 'Lynne had done a great deal for Mum earlier on,' he said.

Gill dearly loved Margaret but couldn't afford the move back to Australia. She also described loving her life in Manchester: 'It was an autonomous and wonderfully exciting role,' she said.

Gill would phone Jim semi-regularly to keep in touch, though their accounts of their phone conversations differ. Gill said she often described what she was doing in her role 'and how much it excited her', and that Jim mentioned on numerous occasions that it would be useful having her do similar work for him. Jim barely recalls talking about her job, though he was aware she had some sort of administration role.

'Our conversations were all about how she felt trapped in the UK and couldn't afford to move back,' Jim said. In 2011 he offered her a job and $20 000 for moving costs. Jim said there was

> a written agreement that if the job didn't work out the debt would be forgiven. I figured that at the worst she'd be back in Australia, could find another job and could spend time with Mum. And to be perfectly honest, the advantage of doing it that way was that the $20 000 became a business expense. I certainly wouldn't normally pay $20 000 moving costs to someone who wasn't my sister, but I wanted Mum to have her company.

The original idea had been for Gill to work at Foothills, but by the time Gill had landed in Melbourne Jim said he would find her a different role. To Gill it was unsettling to suddenly be told she wouldn't have the role she'd accepted. Jim wouldn't comment on this except to say that 'it was Li's decision at that time'. Gill was offered a job setting up a debt collection division despite thinking it wouldn't work, and when this proved correct she was given various roles in compliance and finance.

Gill recounted that a particular woman working there at the time 'started telling Jim I was being rude to her,' Gill said. 'Jim would listen to one person and wouldn't bother with the other side. He'd just react.' Fortunately Gill had saved the emails proving she wasn't the one being rude, and Jim was satisfied. Gill recounted multiple people in the office complaining about her being bossy, when all she'd asked was 'as a matter of courtesy, people turn up to meetings so that we can all get on and do our jobs'.

The end result was that on 14 February 2012, Gill received a redundancy notice. I interviewed numerous people about this, and all said Gill wasn't a good match with the company for numerous reasons, though they wouldn't get into details. Jim gave her different roles trying to find something that worked for everyone, but when they didn't work out he ultimately made the decision to fire her.

> It's our practice to try people in different jobs if one doesn't work out. Firing is the last resort, especially since someone can fail in one job and be brilliant in the next. Unfortunately, Gill didn't work out. I was very disappointed, because I know she's smart and has held other responsible jobs.

He reflected and added,

> I brought her back to Melbourne to be with Mum and I'm not sorry I did, though I probably could have handled it better. It didn't work out very well between us, but at least my mother had somebody else in those last couple of years. She'd had a hard life and she sacrificed so much for us.

Indeed, it was Gill who was at their mother's bedside when she passed away.

For Gill, being fired by her own brother was incredibly upsetting:

> A few days later I had a franchisor say, 'We heard he's shafted you as well, did you hear he's been telling people he sacked you because you're incompetent?' So I got in contact with a reporter from the *Herald Sun* who put it in a little article.

She approached the Fair Work Ombudsman a couple of weeks later, but they explained she would have to go through a legal process to fight her termination and Gill didn't want the stress of it. 'So, I chose not to,' she said.

Gill worked hard to find another job but soon ran out of savings and went on unemployment benefits. 'I got so depressed I went to a local doctor. It was situational depression; I had no money, I had no income,' Gill recalled, seething,

> I was living next door to Jim. He knew I had no money, he knew I didn't have any food in the house, and he didn't even say, 'We bought two loaves of bread, do you want one?'

Jim said he had no idea she was struggling so much.

> How could I know? She'd made it absolutely clear she didn't want to speak to me. She was too angry to even send an email. If she had I certainly would have helped, I've done it often enough in the past.

Jim's daughter Sarah, who gets on well with her aunt Gill, said,

> I don't think he would ever allow someone to go hungry, but I think he would do those actions unknowingly, like terminating her contract. It was a contract, so she didn't have anything else going on.

After two months of unsuccessful job hunting Gill heard from *Today Tonight*. They had seen the *Herald Sun* article and wanted to run her story, saying they would pay her. She did the interview and was told 'you get paid when it airs' — but she didn't know when that would be. Eventually, after five months of job hunting, Gill was successful in getting a job, which was a big relief and helped her out of her situational depression. The *Today Tonight* interview aired 'the Friday of the first week I started the job,' Gill said, and she was paid, though she was not happy with how they spun the story. Gill now works in a permanent role as a manager in a 'totally different industry that I am thoroughly enjoying, and making a difference'.

The last time Jim and Gill saw each other was the start of 2018, at their cousin Lisa's wedding reception, which Jim put on at Foothills and paid for. 'It was a good chance to get the wider family together,' Jim said. 'I went up to Gill and nodded a greeting, which she barely responded to. That was that.'

Jim doesn't hold grudges, but he won't try too hard to mend fences. 'I'm kind of a reflector,' he said.

If somebody likes me, I like them. With Li and the kids, it's very intense both ways. But when somebody's negative, I let them alone. I'm always here, if Gill ever wants to make contact. I was very fond of my little sister and still am. We always had a good bond until this happened, and I hope one day we'll reconcile. I've also made it quite clear that I don't blame her for the TV thing. She was in a tough position and needed the money.

14

Revolt in the Ranks

From 2004 to 2009 eight new divisions started, with three — Earthworks, Windscreens and Graffiti Solutions — no longer operating today. The five still running are Bin Cleaning, Financial Services (formally Finance Professionals), Plumbing, Resurfacing (formerly Bath Resurfacing) and Skip Bins. By 2009 there were 2500 franchisees in the Jim's Group, a mammoth achievement. Jim's was much larger than any of its competitors, but discontent was rising.

Most franchise systems don't have the layer of franchisor or divisional; there is only the corporate office. In these systems the horror stories of franchisees being mistreated are prolific.

Jim lets many things be decided by vote that in other systems would simply be imposed, which is perhaps one reason the Jim's Group has a remarkably low rate of litigation. But it does not mean there are no conflicts or disputes. Regional and divisional franchises can have a significant value, in the hundreds of thousands and even millions of dollars, which gives franchisors and divisionals a vested interest in every decision. And some decisions, especially those involved with service issues, are not subject to vote.

Franchisor frustrations

Jim has the power to 'breach' (give warning that a problem must be resolved) or terminate a divisional, franchisor or franchisee. If he terminates a franchisor or divisional their business is normally put up for sale for six months, and if there are no buyers Jim will often buy it himself. But coming to an agreement on how much the business is worth is tricky, and can lead to some big disputes.

Also, if Jim believes a franchisor is not treating franchisees fairly (or a divisional their franchisors), he may remind franchisees or franchisors of the vote-out clause. He sees this as care for the underdog, but for the franchisors and divisionals, this interference is often very upsetting.

Some franchisors explained that one or two 'rogue' franchisees complained to Jim, and suddenly Jim was calling all their franchisees to remind them of the vote-out clause. They had spent months and years building good relationships, and it didn't feel good to have Jim himself undermining them. Of course, they could see that some franchisors and divisionals have actually done the wrong thing, but Jim's quick reaction to just one or two phone calls, without due diligence, really upsets them.

Jim explained that in most cases where a franchisee contacts him he supports the franchisor because

they usually know what they are doing...But if the case sounds reasonable then I will check up, which may mean phoning and asking other people. And if there is a real problem I can come down hard. I have an abrupt style, which is why others mostly look after franchisors these days.

As Haydar Hussein, the divisional of Jim's Cleaning, explained,

> The divisionals, in some cases, pay millions of dollars for their business. They are powerful people in their own right, yet they still have this concern that they can 'get into trouble', get told off or breached by Jim, at any time. For someone to have the capacity to purchase a multimillion-dollar business, you must be a strong, successful person. In my circle nobody can talk down to me, I won't allow them to. Whereas, unfortunately, Jim can. He can tell me off.

He added that it's fair enough you can get breached,

> because we are bound by the rules of our contract. The only scary thing is that sometimes things happen outside of your control, or by accident or human nature. We're all human, we can all make a wrong decision.

Craig Pritchard is one of three divisional managers employed by Jim to support the divisionals. True to Jim's style, there have been frequent staff changes in the divisional manager role over the years. 'The turnover wouldn't have been ideal for the divisionals, having to build new relationships again. And within divisional managers you would have had different levels of support and engagement,' Craig acknowledged.

A number of people I interviewed explained that Jim himself is not good with the 'carrot'. He knows how to use the 'stick', implementing fines or breaches if someone does the wrong thing, but he doesn't know how to give emotional support or to encourage. He explained that this is why he employs three divisional managers to do that job for him. Finding great divisional managers took some time, with frequent staff changes — and things are still in flux today — but many of the franchisors I interviewed shared they feel far more supported now.

Benn Ward, who has been a franchisor since 2003, said, 'Jim's major focus is on his franchisees, so franchisors are often the middle, and he'll go hard at us if we're not looking after them'.

Phil Maunder, a former state franchisor, said that Jim would

> say that he puts franchisees first...but in reality he actually doesn't. He will put a franchisee first if the franchisee is 100 per cent compliant...But if that franchisee is...let's say he's 90 to 99 per cent compliant, that guy is completely out of the window. And he'd treat that person like they're, effectively, almost like they're criminal, because they are not compliant with the system.

When Jim does discover a franchisor or divisional who has done something dodgy he reacts quickly. 'And we're all painted with the same brush,' Anthony Silverman said. 'So we all get penalised,' he sighed. He gave the example of a certain access franchisors used to have in FMS (Jim's Franchise Management System software) and, after one franchisor did something wrong with that access, 'they took the access away from all of us. Take it away from him, not us too. Now, everybody is restricted,' Anthony said.

He added that, with the size of the Jim's Group,

> I suppose it's a difficult thing to manage. It's easy for me to say this is a problem, but I don't see all the problems they have to deal with. Most of us don't do the wrong thing, but when they see one or two they wonder how many people are doing this. And they don't know unless they investigate everybody. There's Jim's side of it too.

On top of these frustrations, some grumble that their fees are too high and the call centre costs them too much.

In fact, discontent about Jim even resulted in some unpleasant material about Jim being published in 2012, including a book called *50 Shades of Jim*, written by 'Mrs Jimbo, Jim's Nemesis'. It was a scathing review of Jim. It was a mixture of truths and untruths. A number of claims were clearly vindictive and ficticious, but not all: Jim's sister Gill contributed a chapter, honestly sharing her side of the story, and there were emails in the book that seemed genuine. (I was able to read the book — which has been removed from all platforms — thanks to Gill lending me her copy.)

Taking everything into account

While many franchisors agree with all of these issues, and feel they are not supported properly by National Office and only receive 'all stick and no carrot', I also spoke with many franchisors who just love the business. They love the work they do and respect Jim's passion for exceptional customer service, and they understand that Jim is the way he is; 'There's no point getting upset,' many said. Jim is black-and-white and reactionary, and sometimes it would be nice if he could see more grey — but they respect what he's built, and prosper from it. They described Jim as being incredibly helpful and supportive in helping them grow their business.

Sharon Connell, divisional of Jim's Dog Wash, said, 'I'll stay with Jim's forever. He's a good person, very inspirational, and it's been fantastic. I'm not going anywhere, ever. It's the best thing for me'. She went on to say,

> Jim is passionate, and so approachable. I call him and he always has the time, no matter what is going on. He will answer the phone and give great advice, it's amazing.

Paul Sandles, the divisional of Jim's Diggers, explained a time when as a franchisor he had one franchisee complaining to Jim, 'and Jim told the guy, "You're a lone voice. I'm getting nothing but praise from everyone else".' In this instance Jim wasn't reactionary or suspicious of Paul; he could see that it was just one person. Another time Paul wasn't logging his proactive calls to franchisees in FMS, 'and Jim was fine, he coached me,' Paul said.

> He explained, 'You've got to write down your proactive calls. It's in the contract. If you have a problem franchisee they will find any small thing they can to trip you up'. I feel very supported by Jim — I know I can call him up if I've got a question, especially a curly one.

Nicole Wood, a Cleaning franchisor, said Jim 'has been a generous man. He is really passionate about his brand, and he genuinely wants people to succeed'.

In every business decision Jim makes, there are five parties he considers: the customer, franchisee, franchisor, divisional and the Jim's brand as a whole. Haydar Hussein, the divisional of Cleaning, spoke of many times he's gone to Jim with a question and received an unexpected answer.

'When you ask him a question, he is smart enough to analyse the five different areas and give you the right answer within seconds,' Haydar said. It may not always be the answer Haydar was looking for, but after going away and thinking it through, he would come to understand why, when all five are taken into account, that was the right decision, even if it didn't feel good to Haydar.

UK troubles

In 2009 Paul Carr was the divisional in the UK. In July of that year Jim received an email with a list of concerns about Paul Carr. Among them were complaints of a lack of training and support, and that the promised ads had not been placed in a local paper for some time. I was unfortunately unable to obtain contact details for Paul Carr.

Jim says that a consultant working for National Office investigated the complaints, and emailed him with the opening line: 'There is no doubt that Paul's support is lacking'. Jim did some further research by contacting most of the UK franchisees, 'and their account was much the same,' Jim said. Jim emailed Shirley Harry, who was working in documents at the time:

> Shirley
> Can you do breaches for Paul Carr or his company for:
>   Jim's Mowing (Norfolk) Region
>   Divisional Franchise
>   Failure to pay fees on time
>   Failure to provide proper support such as pro-active calls, notes taken, and responding promptly and helpfully to Franchisor/Franchisee enquiries
> Jim

According to Jim, heated emails were exchanged between him and Paul. Jason Jaap, who'd grown Jim's Mowing in the UK and sold his franchisor rights to Paul, had a different take on the situation. But by the time Jason rang Jim to try and explain what could actually be happening, Jim was adamant. Jason recalled,

I tried to explain to Jim that it might not be the way he saw it, but I think he'd had pretty heated words with Paul and Paul said some words back, and as far as Jim was concerned Paul was evil and he had to go — Jim had made his mind up.

Jim said that 'It was clear to me that Paul wasn't doing the job, and didn't intend to, and failure to support franchisees gets me pretty upset. So I had Paul terminated'.

Jason said,

Paul said and did a lot of things that didn't help his position and certainly wasn't wise from a business perspective ... Paul had a lot of reason to take the actions he took; he put a lot of money into getting Jim's Mowing working in the UK.

Paul Carr commissioned a survey on whether Jim should remain in charge, sending it to all the franchisors. Of the 215-odd who responded, around forty said they wanted Jim gone. This was passed to the media, resulting in a story written by Chalpat Sonti in *The Sydney Morning Herald* in October 2009 and titled 'Turfed out: Jim's Mowing magnate faces the sack'. Chalpat Sonti wrote that 'Jim's Group allows franchisors to be voted out by franchisees — or Mr Penman to be voted out by franchisors — if three people call for a referendum'.[1] Jim asserts that, according to the Jim's Group contracts, this isn't true: there is no legal way Jim as national franchisor could be voted out, though he could be voted out as a regional or divisional franchisor. Nonetheless, the story was taken up by a number of other Fairfax publications, and even the ABC did a radio segment on it, with Simon Santow interviewing Warren Smith, Chris Munday and Jim.

Among all the heat there were franchisors strongly opposed to voting Jim out, though others, like Anthony Silverman, would have liked to have had a proper vote.

> Jim said he would do a vote, but only if it included franchisees voting as well as franchisors. But the franchisees wouldn't vote him out because they wouldn't understand all the problems. They didn't know half of it.

Silvia Valeri began working at National Office in June 2009, so had only been there a few months when things got heated. I asked her what she thought of that time.

> When you start here you have to not listen to everything that's going on. You have to put your own perspective on things, because you'll have franchisees saying things, franchisors saying things, staff saying things, and then Jim would come in and have a chat to you as well. I just gathered all the information together and went, 'Okay, this is what I think about it,' and kept my mouth shut. I didn't think much of it.

All the disgruntled talk went nowhere, with no legal mechanism for a vote-out to occur. An item on the advisory meeting agenda of 13 November 2009 was a 'Proposal to appoint a CEO and a Board of Directors to manage the Jim's Group'. What came out of this, as noted in the minutes, was an agreement that Jim would appoint staff to act in a coordination role between franchisors and himself.

The committee also asked that the Mowing divisional manager not be overloaded with other matters, which meant appointing someone else to look after the other divisions. 'They had a fair point,' Jim agreed. 'We were demanding better support for franchisees but not giving them the best support.' Over the years support staff have increased, to the extent that by the end of 2018 National Office had three divisional managers, two supporting admin staff, and Jim, all providing active support for both franchisors and franchisees. 'This is a long way from the single manager I had back in 2009,' Jim said.

Another agenda item at that advisory meeting was 'Voting out Jim as owner'. At the meeting Jim again made his point that any vote must include franchisees, since many of the issues involved him supporting franchisees over franchisors. The action item simply read: 'No action and no legal basis. Jim will not be stepping down.'

The minutes of this meeting make interesting reading. The members agreed that Jim's passion and drive were valuable and should be retained, but they wanted better support and fewer capricious changes.

'I don't have anything in principle against being voted out if I'm not doing my job, which was why we did the referendum four years earlier,' Jim said.

> But I was quite annoyed by those articles. They upset potential buyers and lost us franchise sales. I was naive enough in those days to be shocked that major newspapers would print a story which ten minutes' research would have shown to be false.

Jim asked about suing Fairfax but was advised against it.

> I was told they would interview every disgruntled ex-franchisee and ex-franchisor and spread the dirt. It was just not worth it. So for

the next ten years I simply exercised my right as a business owner to reject every Fairfax advertising proposal that came across my desk. Considering how many millions of dollars we've spent on advertising since then, it may have been the most expensive article Fairfax ever published.

Though the idea of Jim being voted out was incorrect reporting, the discontent among franchisors was not. In his article Chalpat stated the franchisors had concerns regarding 'changes to the company's operational manual', which was true. When there were a lot of changes to the manual it caused upset, because their contracts often referred to the manual. As Craig Parke explained,

> Jim couldn't change the contract without us agreeing, but he could change the manual any time he wanted to. So he changed the manual and the contract said 'as per manual', and therefore he changed the contract.

Changes were being brought in, such as a requirement for franchisors to phone their franchisees at least monthly, called 'proactive calls'. 'Franchisees liked it and most franchisors could see the sense,' Jim said. 'Those who did it lost fewer franchisees and grew faster. But they didn't want it made compulsory.'

The discontent among franchisors, according to Craig, 'went on and on and on, for a long time'. It came to a head at the same advisory meeting, where, after a heated discussion, it was agreed that any future changes to the franchisor manual be put to referendum and rejected if a majority were against it. Later it was decided that the advisory committee itself could reject any proposed change, before it went to referendum. These changes were written into the manual.

'I realised I had been pushing too hard,' Jim said,

and the new process works quite well. We don't always progress as fast as I'd like, but the system has continued to tighten over the years and franchisee support is far better now.

In 2018 the same right was offered to franchisees, who can now veto changes to their own manual. All subsequent changes have been approved by majority vote.

Chalpat quoted Jim as saying, 'And if they [the franchisors] all want to take a class action against me, they can go ahead'. Interestingly, there is a fund that has been going for many years that some franchisors contribute to regularly, so if they ever need to take legal action against Jim, they can afford a proper fight. Jim is very aware of this fund. 'I don't mind them having it, but I am very confident they'll never use it,' he said. To date this has proved correct, though Jim's relationship with franchisors is still not always rosy. The perception is that when an issue arises Jim always takes the side of the franchisee, and his black-and-white nature and abrupt communication style have not helped franchisors feel Jim is looking out for them.

Craig Parke was a divisional in 2009 and was at this eventful advisory meeting. He said, 'Paul Carr didn't really affect us. He got press, but guys on the ground weren't really affected at all'. Craig explained that the unrest was there anyway.

Legal proceedings

In March 2010 *The Sydney Morning Herald* [2] published an article, again written by Chalpat Sonti, stating that Paul Carr filed a statement of claim in the High Court in London claiming Jim Penman, Phil Maunder and Richard Harrison 'acted in concert to remove' him. That same day *InvestSMART*[3] published an article stating that

> Mr Carr said he was preparing a defamation action against Mr Penman. 'I am also now, having got this far, not interested in any settlement he may eventually decide to offer,' Mr Carr said.

The article went on to say that 'Mr Penman earlier offered Mr Carr 80 per cent of the value of the business'.

Jim retaliated by launching a defamation case against Paul Carr in the Victorian Supreme Court, 'where I won,' Jim said, 'but in the end I thought, "This is stupid". I emailed Paul and started a dialogue'. Jim forgave the money owed in the defamation case, and offered to pay him '$50 000 for the division. Which was a fair enough price, and what we should have done much, much earlier. I let my anger get control of me,' Jim said.

Jim recalled this whole ordeal with regret.

> It was one of the stupidest things I ever did, getting so angry instead of keeping in contact with Paul and coming to a fair resolution. Paul had a fair point and, in retrospect, I admire his guts in fighting it so hard.

When Paul Carr had bought Jason Jaap's share of Jim's Mowing in the UK in 2006 there had been ten franchisees operating. By January 2009 Paul had built it up to twenty-nine franchisees, an impressive feat in a country where the brand wasn't, and still isn't, well known. But by January 2010 things had declined, with franchisee numbers dropping back to twenty-two. The UK remains a tough market for the Jim's Group, with Cleaning and Dog Wash attempting to launch there in recent years, but not gaining much traction. In December 2018 there were only sixteen Jim's Mowing franchisees in the UK. Some still hope to make a big success of Jim's there, but it is yet to be accomplished.

Jim's legal strategy

Franchising tends to lead to more disputes than general business. Franchisees invest their own money in their business, but can still be dictated to by the corporate office, sometimes in ways that affect their bottom line, which can cause upset. And in the Jim's Group there are the extra layers of franchisors and divisionals. However the Jim's Group has only been to court a handful of times in twenty-nine years. There have been far more disputes that Jim has settled before they reached litigation, but, even so, the number of disputes is low for a franchise of its size. In 2017 the Jim's Group had only a couple of notices of dispute from franchisees, which, considering the almost 4000 franchisees, is a tiny amount. Jim explained, 'If somebody's got a genuine issue and I think they've got any rights to it, I just fix it. We've very rarely gone to court'.

With everything the Senate inquiry into the franchising industry in Australia is bringing to light, it is clear the Jim's Group is an anomaly in the industry. Because Jim puts his franchisees first and so passionately cares about their welfare and success, franchisee legal issues have been minor. It is usually the franchisors or divisionals who get lawyers involved.

Jim's strategy for running a legal dispute is to make it cost the other side more than it costs him.

I do it deliberately. My in-house lawyer writes letter after letter, deliberately pushing up their legal fees. I just keep fighting and making their life difficult and expensive until they eventually come to terms, usually for what we offered in the first place. I don't want to paint myself as being an angel because I'm not. I take advantage of the legal system.

Later he added that he does

always try to be fair, keep the emotion out of it and never back people into a corner. I mediate at every opportunity, but if I have to fight, I fight hard.

Jim is very transparent about his way of operating, to the extent that he won't accept confidentiality clauses so he can tell people what he's done. 'I want people to know what happens when you fight me,' Jim said.

I'm a pretty hard fighter, I mean I wouldn't take me on if I wasn't me. I want to do the right thing, but I can't be weak because you become a target. I'll do my best to treat people fairly but if you make me an enemy, it's going to hurt you.

For most, litigation is a very traumatic and emotional process that takes its toll — but Jim isn't affected by law suits (his time in the family court was a scarring exception).

Though Jim knows the legal system well, he despises it. 'The legal system is so stacked in the favour of the wealthy because justice is so complicated and long-winded and most can't afford to go to court,' Jim said. 'It's terrible. I hate it. Lawyers make a fortune, and everyone else suffers.'

Paradoxically, Jim's hatred for the unfairness of the legal system has never stopped him using it to his advantage.

> We take extraordinary care to make sure people are treated fairly. When we terminate a regional franchisor, for example, we sell the business and give the money to them. But if you do the wrong thing, and then you take me to court — I will win.

Jim recalled a case where a woman had bought a franchise and was let down by her franchisor. Jim wrote to her saying she should get her money back from the franchisor. Tragically, the woman passed away. Her husband took up the case, 'but rather than coming to me for help, they decided they'd take me on because I have deep pockets,' Jim said. 'Which is typical of lawyers, but idiotic thinking.' So Jim did what he always does, forcing the costs up. It got to mediation and was settled, with them getting $35 000 back, plus an extra $5000.

Later, Jim found out that it cost them $100 000 in legal fees just to get to mediation.

> It was appalling! It's such an evil system. This whole family's wealth was destroyed! What the lawyers should have done is looked at the case and said, 'The national franchiser is on your side, get him to help you'. But they just milked money out of the husband, charging him $100 000 in fees when all they got back for him was $40 000!

Jim, in a mediation in 2018, told the party fighting him, 'I will bleed you white'. He doesn't shy away from intimidation tactics to force people to settle, a strategy that often works — because he's not bluffing.

Jim was careful to explain that he 'has only ever been to court with a franchisor three times':

> One was an ex-franchisor who didn't get as much for his business from a third party as he wanted. Another was an action taken against a divisional franchisor on behalf of the franchisors and at their request. And the third was when I sued someone for libel ... All were settled out of court.

15

Tackling Insurance

The Jim's franchise is usually thought of as only offering trade services, but there are some professional service divisions as well. There is Jim's Bookkeeping, Jim's Financial Services, Jim's Real Estate and Jim's Insurance.

Jim used different insurers over the years as preferred suppliers for his franchisees, negotiating the best rate possible, but still found their service lacking. The Jim's Group is large and complicated, with the different divisions and different layers of franchisees, franchisors, divisionals and National Office. 'Other brokers just couldn't get it. There were complaints and claims weren't getting done,' Jim said.

A frantic start

In an effort to give his franchisees the best rates possible, in 2010 Jim decided to start his own insurance company by getting a broker licence and bringing it in house. A great idea, but, like many of Jim's ideas, when put into practice it proved far more challenging than he'd anticipated. Jim tried two managers, neither of whom worked out. In

November 2010 Jim offered his son Andrew, who had been working as a compliance manager at National Office for the previous year, the challenge, along with the reward of a substantial amount of money if he could pull it off. It was an unfair ask of Andrew, who had no prior experience in the insurance industry. Still, Andrew dived into the role.

After obtaining a broker's licence they realised that roughly 800 franchisees lacked public liability insurance, despite it being compulsory in the contract. 'With one accident we could have been sued for millions, and so could the franchisee and the franchisor. No-one could afford that,' Jim said.

So in February 2011 Jim announced through the newsletter that everyone must use Jim's Insurance for public risk, so he could check everyone actually had it, and there was an uproar. Jim ploughed ahead, and after the switch to using Jim's Insurance was made they breached operators who didn't get it due to the risk they posed to the whole group.

By August 2011 the strain took its toll on Andrew, who quit, though he wouldn't go into any detail as to why. Jim simply said, 'I put him into a job way over his head. He gave it everything he had but didn't have the experience and got very stressed by it'.

I asked Jim why he had given his son such an impossible task in the first place. 'I always had a vision for my sons to be in the business,' Jim said.

After Andrew's departure Jim's Insurance, again, needed a new manager, and in October 2011 Jadran Sango was interviewed for the job. Jadran has been an insurance broker since 1989, the same year Jim launched the franchise. Acquaintances in the insurance industry told Jadran, "'Don't work for Jim. He's mad, they've had four different managers,'" Jadran recalled.

Jadran's interview was on a Sunday at Jim's home, and he arrived to find Li and the kids around. He was surprised by how casual it was and how nice Jim seemed. 'Driving home I was thinking, "What are these people saying about Jim?" But it was a Sunday and he was in a relaxed mood.'

Though Jadran had enjoyed the interview, he didn't accept the role because his father had passed away three months before and he didn't feel ready for a big change. However a week into January Jim's recruiter called. All the insurance policies were set to be renewed in April, and they really needed a good manager to get it across the line. Jadran decided to accept the role, knowing that the April renewal would be sink or swim. He would have two staff to assist.

Jadran gave notice at work and booked a family holiday to the Gold Coast to relax before starting at Jim's Insurance in March. While on a ride at the Gold Coast Jadran's phone rang — it was Jim. 'I just wanted to let you know the two others have resigned, do you know anyone?'

'What?!' Jadran exclaimed.

'They've resigned.'

'That's not good…'

'Do you know anyone?' Jim asked again.

Luckily Jadran did. While still in a rubber boat on the ride he called a woman he knew would be great, Sally Martin, and she accepted the job offer. They began together in March, working with Joel, a young man in his twenties who had been doing some casual work in another department and 'was still learning insurance,' Jadran said. (Joel went on to become Operations Manager, and then Chief Digital Officer.) 'That was the team. I don't know how it would have gone if Sally said no….' Jadran remarked.

They only had five weeks until renewals. Jadran focused on mending relationships with in-house staff, franchisors, franchisees and others in the industry. Jim visited every day to hear how they were going, pushing Jadran hard and telling him he had his support every step of the way. 'Just do what you have to do to make it work. If you have roadblocks from other departments, or anywhere, tell me and I'll make it happen,' Jim said.

Jadran set to work. There was a backlog of claims to be sorted out, and policies and processes to be put in place so legitimate claims could be paid out quickly. 'If a Jim's franchisee loses their tools, they need to be back on the road right away,' Jadran explained.

Jadran's first two years were 'Operation Repair', as he called it. It is now in its sixth year and doing well. 'We work pretty closely with Jim still, on ideas on how we can improve,' Jadran said.

> For me having the support of Jim and Li is great. They are obviously busy but they always find time to chat. I have worked in other organisations where you have to line up to see the CEO, or make an appointment in two weeks' time. Here there is no red tape, you have direct access.

Jim's Insurance is very different from most brokers. Normally underwriters and brokers are separate, and there is no incentive to reduce risk because premiums are spread widely. But Jim's Insurance works with underwriters to reduce claims. 'We act to keep next year's premiums down,' Jim said. An example of this is how they handle the depreciation of equipment. Initially the underwriters treated year-old mowers as brand new, and 'we were getting all these claims of mowers disappearing after about a year,' Jim chuckled.

From my own experience mowing lawns, I know a contractor's year-old mower is worth practically nothing. We told the underwriters to put in a steep depreciation, and it immediately got rid of most of those kinds of claims.

Jadran explained that 'it's a very unique brokerage. There's no other two-way brokers out there, looking after both interests'.

This proximity to the Jim's Group means that fair claims are paid fast. 'We won't knock back someone on a stupid technicality because we represent the franchisees,' Jim said. 'We want to stop false claims to keep premiums down, but genuine claims are paid quickly.' If a loss is claimed in the morning the franchisee will have their money by that afternoon or the next day. It's all decided within the brokerage.

I asked Jim how they know whether a claim is authentic. 'It's not difficult,' he said,

because we know our people pretty well. We know their customer service record, their financial issues, their character, how many leads they're taking. Ninety-nine per cent are great people and there is no question at all.

I asked Jadran what it's like working for Jim. 'Taking this job was the best thing I've ever done,' Jadran said. 'Jim is tough but fair; if you do the right thing you are looked after.' While researching this book I attended a Friday staff lunch at Foothills. A buffet of eight main dishes, salads, a fruit and cheese platter, and sweet treats were laid out. Jim was there, eating at a table with his young son Aaron and a nephew. The only staff member to join Jim's table was Jadran.

'There are people who, when they see Jim, walk the other way,' Jadran said. 'I think employees should get to know Jim a bit more.'

Too trusting

Jim does develop strong bonds with some staff. Shirley Harry began working for Jim in October 1997, and recalled she 'said hello to him and he just looked at me and walked off,' Shirley laughed.

> So I purposely made an effort to go up to his desk and say hello — so he couldn't run away! He'd just stare and then eventually say hello. After a while he started to talk and joke around with me. A few times he mentioned he saw himself as a father figure to me, which was strange. But he respected my ethics and the way I worked.

Shirley began her work at Jim's answering the phones, and when she worked weekends he would 'bring all his kids in. He was very involved with them. He loves children,' she recalled.

In 2003 Shirley was working in the contracts department. Her main job was to prepare contracts, disclosure documents and any documents the franchisors needed. Often franchisors asked for changes to be made to 'schedules, fee structures, pay for work guarantees, things like that,' Shirley said, which she didn't feel comfortable doing. She told her manager her concern, but 'he was very orientated on what the franchisors wanted', so instead she went to Jim to check he was okay with those changes being made, since they would affect Jim's commission, 'and it wasn't fair that one group of franchisees were paying more fees than someone else,' Shirley said.

Jim totally trusted the manager and told Shirley to do what the manager had said. He let all the changes through so again, she went to Jim. Shirley told Jim,

> I don't feel comfortable with this, because it's not fair. We now have one franchisor who's got his own fee structure separate to everyone

else. We're allowing franchisors to enter information onto our system, and I've checked a few and they're putting in their own fees, not what's in your contract.

This got Jim's attention. They blocked the franchisors' access to putting in fees, and as contracts expired made sure all the new ones were correct, with everyone having the same fee structure.

Jim is someone who believes in the good of people, until proven otherwise. He trusts they will do the right thing, as when he hired Jadran and immediately entrusted him with the entire insurance endeavour. A common theme that all of his long-serving staff shared was that he is far too trusting; of staff, managers, divisionals, franchisors and franchisees. He has been ripped off countless times. Li mentioned she caught staff re-submitting the same receipt for reimbursement more than once when working in the finance department. There were debts being written off without any written consent or paper trail, just a verbal order from a manager without Jim's consent or knowledge. There have been personal expenses slipped in on company expenses. There was an accountant who had the Jim's Group continue paying his phone bill for over a year after leaving Jim's — Jill Stallworthy found this one, and proudly cut off the service. 'But at that time there was no exit strategy when people left the company, so it was partly our fault,' Jill added.

Jim's Group began as a small business and grew, but it was often chaotic, as many businesses are, with systems and processes not yet in place to stop cheating from happening. Franchisors, franchisees and divisionals alike would find loopholes in the system to pay Jim far less than what they were meant to, and exploit it. Today the Jim's Group has far tighter control, but it took many years of plugging the holes to stop the leaking of cash. I asked Jim if it upset him to be cheated so many times. 'I don't care that they've ripped me off but I do care that they've ripped off my franchisees as well,' Jim said. Tino Grossi said Jim has told him exactly the same thing on many occasions: 'I don't care if I don't get my money back, but you better get their money back.'

I asked Shirley if Jim is partly to blame for being stolen from, and she immediately said, 'He's too trusting. It's one thing I've always said to him'. Tino said that Jim's weaknesses are that 'he trusts too many people and he's very soft', a characterisation some would be shocked by.

Benn Ward commented that Jim 'does have extreme faith in his staff; once he puts someone into a position he will back them until he decides they're no longer suited for the role'.

Jim agreed that he is too trusting. He explained that dishonest and incapable people soon reveal themselves, and that when you do find good staff, trusting them from the start helps. 'I have an unusual number of dedicated staff who seem to care more about my money than I do,' Jim chuckled. These staff members have helped plug many of the holes. 'Most of my staff are dedicated — I'm incredibly lucky to have them.'

16

Looking for The One

One of Jim's key problems over the years has been his failure to find a great second-in-command. He freely admits he doesn't have everything it takes to run the company properly, neither the administration skills to oversee staff nor the personal skills to keep people happy. 'The issues in 2009' — the general unrest and call for a vote out — 'are an example of the problems that arise without a good right-hand man in charge,' Jim said. It was in an effort to resolve this that in early 2014 Jim invited Neil Welsh and James Jacka to become partners with him. They bought a 10 per cent stake in the Jim's Group.

An acrimonious partnership

Neil Welsh first joined Jim's Test and Tag in May 2004 as a franchisor, and it later became evident that the couple running Test and Tag were struggling. 'In those days we simply looked for people who were running a successful business in the field — there were a lot of failures,' Jim said. He realised the founders weren't up to the task, so he rang Neil. Neil built a business plan around the opportunity, and Neil and his partner, James Jacka, bought the Test and Tag division. Together they did an exceptional job running it.

So good that, in 2007, Jim offered Neil a part-time job at National Office. Neil declined. This offer was made a few times over the years, with Neil actually coming into the office for two days at one point, before declining and continuing running Test and Tag with James.

Jim was very impressed with their work, writing in *Every Customer a Raving Fan* that

> Neil and James put in place the most rigorous systems of selection, training and support, achieving the lowest levels of attrition and one of the lowest levels of complaints. As a result it grew steadily, year after year, and is now our third largest division.

Jim wanted to replicate Test and Tag's extensive manuals, rigorous selection process, documentation and great support into the other divisions. He did, eventually, succeed in bringing Neil into National Office, with Neil later becoming Chief Operating Officer (COO) for a time. I interviewed Neil for this book, but he asked not to be quoted.

In early 2014 Neil and James became Jim's partners, buying a 10 per cent stake in the Jim's Group. It was the first time Jim had ever sold a percentage of his stake in the Jim's Group.

However, the partnership did not last long. Staff I interviewed, including Jadran from Jim's Insurance, told me what they saw happen. Jadran said, 'Neil set to work with the goal to really grow Jim's Group. To do this he hired multiple managers in various roles, and they were big money with no return in sight'.

Tino Grossi was a Skip Bins franchisor who was helping out in the office at that time. He said Neil was trying to create a position for every little thing. He created a marketing team and everyone was on big money. They were going backwards — as a businessman I could see it.

Jadran was one of the people who alerted Jim to what was happening. 'I could see with my own eyes it just wasn't right,' Jadran said. 'I had to jump in. I told Jim, "Mate, you've got to look at this".' Tino gave Jim the same warning, telling him,

'Jim, you can tell me to mind my own business but please be careful with the amount of money that's leaving — I don't see extra money coming in. I think it's spiralling backwards'. But at this point Jim trusted that Neil knew what he was doing, and replied 'No, no, we'll be alright'.

A few weeks later Tino was just about to walk into a weekly marketing meeting when Haydar Hussein, the divisional for Jim's Cleaning, called. Tino remembered Haydar asking:

How do I get in touch with the marketing manager? I'm going to take my money elsewhere rather than Jim's. I mean I want to do the right thing, but I can't get hold of them so how am I supposed to do any marketing with them?

Minutes later that marketing manager walked into the meeting in high spirits. "'I've just secured the deal with Cleaning,'" Tino recalled him announcing. Tino waited for the meeting to finish and then went to Jim.

'Jim, before you go home all happy, go to your office, close the door and ring Haydar,' Tino said.

Jim did, and discovered the marketing manager had lied. Rather than gaining them business, the guy was driving it away. The next day Jim told Neil the man had to go. 'Either you do it or I will. Keep in mind that I own 90 per cent of the business, and you only own 10 per cent.'

The same thing happened with other staff Neil had hired. Jim explained that

Neil appointed a number of people, making the payroll rise alarmingly, but I couldn't see them doing anything useful. Franchisors complained about lack of support and our income was flat. If it kept up we would not be able to pay our bills.

In the end Neil and James were partners with Jim for less than six months.

In April 2018, a couple of months after our interview, Neil and James sent a Notice of Dispute to Jim, claiming damages. Their mediation was unsuccessful, and as of writing nothing has happened since.

Skip Bins stoush

The Skip Bins division was founded by brothers Andrew and Craig Parke in 2007. By then both had been in Jim's for quite some time and knew the system well. '[We] worked out that we were both pretty good at selling franchises,' Andrew Parke said, and they had the idea to run a division together. Craig, who knew Jim better, having worked and travelled with him for years, was the one who approached Jim with the idea for Jim's Skip Bins. 'There was a bit of pushback from the Mowing people because they believed that they had a right to take rubbish away, which they do,' Andrew Parke said. The brothers explained Skip Bins was different from going to a customer's house and loading a trailer with rubbish — it was hiring out traditional skip bins — which calmed people down, and Jim gave them the okay. Andrew purchased 'one skip bin and a truck, and away we went'. They started selling franchises and regional franchises, and the division grew over time.

One prospect for a regional franchise was Tino Grossi, who had made his money as a vegetable farmer. He worked long hours, using the profits to buy one parcel of land after another. At its peak Tino's business employed 72 people and 130 contractors around Australia. One of his key achievements was to create a strain of baby broccoli that is eaten around the world today. 'It took me four years to develop,' Tino said. 'I cross-bred broccoli plants that had long stems.' After intensive effort he had actually given up, throwing the last seeds onto a bare patch of land, only to be informed later that there was a strange sort of plant growing there — baby broccoli! He received plant breeders' royalties for many years, supplying major supermarkets around Australia.

In 2010 Tino received an incredible offer for his land, retiring rich and investing the money in commercial real estate. He never needed to work again, but retirement soon got boring. In April 2013 he bought franchisor rights for Jim's Skip Bins, so he could 'get out of the house and have an interest in something other than my investments,' Tino said.

In 2013, within three months of buying a regional Skip Bins franchise, Tino saw problems with the division. 'I noticed that things weren't right,' Tino said. 'I had caught him [one of the divisionals] thieving the marketing money.'

Tino voiced his concerns, and things came to a head at an advisory meeting where, according to Tino, Craig bad-mouthed Tino (who was not at the meeting). Some of Tino's friends at the meeting 'taped the whole conversation'; Craig 'tried to get the Jim's advisory group to say "Yeah, let's get rid of him",' Tino said, referring to himself.

Jim remembered that 'there were accusations flying all over the place'.

Tino said he would launch a legal case, and according to Tino, Jim responded, 'I don't want it to get to where we go into battle against each other'.

'Well if you buy the [Skip Bins] division,' which would remove the Parke brothers, 'I'll give you my word, I'll stop all legal proceedings,' Tino replied.

Like all stories, there are different perspectives of what happened. Tino explained he was unhappy with the brothers' running of the division because he believed that 'they were stealing about $100 000 a year'.

Craig Parke explained

they accused us of stealing money from an advertising fund, then they got an independent auditor to audit them. I think there was a seven-dollar discrepancy, or something like that. Then they weren't satisfied and they got Jim's head office to audit it they come up with the exact same thing.

Andrew Parke explained it as

a shocking time... Tino Grossi, he absolutely lied, cheated the whole lot, right through that whole thing. And in the end it was over like a five-dollar invoice to Facebook…We approached Jim … it was clear that Jim just didn't want to know and didn't want to hear the truth.

Jim's position was clear:

> For the record, I doubt any money was stolen. One of the key problems was that Craig and his brother Andrew were doing the internet marketing for the division, and it wasn't clear how much margin they were making on the job.

Andrew Parke had a separate software business at the time, which helped with the marketing and search engine optimisation (i.e. how high one ranks on Google) for his divisions. During that time Google rolled out algorithm updates that caused many businesses' Google rankings to drop dramatically, including the Jim's Skip Bins website.

'A lot of websites went from ranking one and two to pretty much ranking on the tenth page,' Andrew explained.

> A lot of the work dried up because of this … Tino decided to blame us at the time, and tried to convince all the franchisors that we were doing something wrong.

For Jim, by this stage, the 'bottom line was that the franchisors were at war with the divisionals, so I did what we always do in these situations: organise a buyout'. National Office 'was the obvious buyer,' Jim said.

Jim rang Craig Parke asking him how much he wanted for the division, and Craig gave his price. 'It was a really messy, messy situation … There was that much bad will and everything else that we just couldn't continue doing business with them,' Craig said. And so Jim bought the division.

'We lost a lot of money,' Craig added. 'And we also owned ... the divisional rights for Jim's Dog Wash at that stage, so that all came to a head as well.'

Jim was pleased to have the problem solved and that Craig and Andrew were getting what he saw as a fair price. 'I've always liked Craig, since I got to know him as this tall young man who helped me out at mowing franchise meetings in the early days,' Jim recalled fondly. 'Overall he made a lot of money from the Jim's Group and we did well out of him. I'm pleased with that.'

However Andrew feels like they were totally mistreated.

**We had folders and folders of evidence and emails and recordings ...
We did nothing wrong. Tino painted the Parke brothers as being
the worst people going around but that's not true.**

At this time Jim wasn't very impressed with Tino: 'I liked him, but thought he was overly emotional'.

Tino said that he and Jim 'had many arguments at the very start. In the end it was to the point where they were going to terminate me, but my franchisees loved me, which made Jim respect what I was doing'.

A new CEO

Tino spent only a few hours a week on his region. It ran smoothly, and he wanted to do more. He offered to help out at National Office, but Jim declined. Soon after Jim saw how well Tino ran his region, despite spending only a few hours a week on it, and accepted Tino's offer to come in part time.

'The results were impressive,' Jim said.

I paid him nothing, about a thousand dollars a month, and he was very effective. He was able to get alongside a franchisor, to be a friend to them, but to also push them to do much better. He could turn around people I would have thought of as hopeless. As soon as I could, I asked him to come into the office full time and help with other divisions as well.

In January 2014 Tino started running the Skip Bins division for Jim as part of his role at National Office. 'At the time it was rife with dispute and doing poorly,' Jim said. 'And three months later, it was one of our best performing divisions!'

Tino recalled that there had been a few people who were still hindering the culture in the division, so he pressured them to sell. The rest were re-energised and brought into the shared vision.

Tino soon started taking on other responsibilities. He brought Jim's attention to staff who were demotivated and not pulling their weight. 'I asked him to see what he could do to re-motivate them, and performance lifted markedly,' Jim said. One staff member was on the verge of being fired, but within a few months she did so well she was given a major raise.

'I was just astonished by this guy,' Jim said. 'He seemed so effective, but I didn't realise at the time that some of his methods would cause problems in the future.'

After some time Jim told Tino, 'You're basically running the place anyway. Do you want to be Chief Operating Officer?' Tino wasn't keen. Being the Jim's Group GM/COO/CEO (Jim is loose with titles) is in many ways considered a 'poisoned chalice', because so many people have been in that role and been fired. But Jim was adamant Tino was perfect for the role, and Tino ended up accepting the title.

By this time he and Jim had become close friends, discovering their values were very aligned. Both are deeply passionate about customer service and service to franchisees, but they had very different skill sets. Tino seemed to be great at communication, and able to manage the complex network of relationships in the Jim's Group so everything ran smoothly.

> Tino was just amazing. I was in awe of his ability to relate to people and he was also incredibly hard working, making calls at all times of the day and night and even when on holiday. I can be a bit lazy and it was so easy to have someone else take care of things. Sometimes I look at myself and I'm astonished I've been successful at all. People don't like talking to me very much. I can give answers to questions and make decisions really fast, but I don't have that personal likeability. I like working on the big picture, coming up with new ideas and focusing on particular issues such as customer service. But I'm not much of a manager. Tino seemed to have everything I lacked.

Soon after Tino became COO, tragedy struck. On Boxing Day 2014 Tino's brother committed suicide; it was a terrible blow to him and his family. Tino decided to resign and retire to spend time at home.

When Tino told Jim he was resigning, Jim replied,

> Stay. I don't care if you don't work at all, but you need people around you, Tino, that's your character. Just come in and talk to people around the office and I'll pay you for it. And when you're feeling up to it I would really like you to take on another division. You're a good person, you're valuable to me.

Tino walked out more committed than ever. 'I drove home and my wife said, "Have you resigned?" and I said, "No I've just taken on more work." She just laughed,' Tino said.

When Tino began working at National Office he was paid a salary of $12 000. 'I don't need the money, I just wanted something to do,' Tino said. In his second year this was doubled to $24 000. Another company offered him $500 000 a year, but he turned it down. 'The work I do at Jim's is helping many people. That job would only help one person,' Tino explained.

In May 2018 Jim formalised Tino's role by making him CEO of Jim's Group, but before long realised that this was 'a serious mistake'.

I had taken him from his area of passion and skill, as a business coach, and into areas that were not his strong point. The direct methods that had worked well with most franchisors were making staff members and some franchisors, especially women, feel threatened. After a few months Tino insisted on stepping back into a coaching role, with the managers he had helped recruit and train stepping in to fill the gap. I owe him a great deal, and so do the many franchisees and franchisors he has helped over the years.

17

Duelling Diggers

From 2010 to 2018 thirty-three Jim's divisions were launched. Unlike in previous phases of growth the overwhelming majority became successful, with only the last six listed no longer in operation. Insurance, Glass, Diggers (formerly Dingos), Termite and Pest Control (formerly Pest Control), Building Inspections, Security, Removals, Conveyancing, Locksmiths, Shade Sails, Traffic Control, Mobile Phones, Heating and Cooling, Window Tinting, Hazardous Material Removal, BBQ Cleaning, Interior Design, Flyscreens and Blinds, Energy, Kitchens, Mobile Cafe, Photography and Drones, Real Estate, Batteries, Drafting and Design, Mobile Tyres, Roller Doors, Bathrooms, Concrete Cutting, Insulation Services, Driving School, Site Solution, and Timber Milling. It is no wonder there are memes all over the internet about Jim's doing every service, with people making up their own — Jim's Exotic Cheeses, Jim's Drug Dealing and Jim's Hand Jobs.

For the number of divisions there are, it is remarkable how well Jim's system manages all parties, making sure quality service is provided by everyone.

Jim and MOTIVATION

There are many reasons why Jim has been so successful, but perhaps the most powerful is his ability to incentivise people to want to do the right thing, and to want to grow their business.

Franchisees pay the same flat fee no matter how big their business gets, which encourages them to grow. The bigger they get, the more money they make, without paying 'a cent more in fees,' Jim said.

Jim motivates franchisors the same way. Franchisors tend to give better support than managers. Rather than have a few people on a salary selling franchises, he lets experienced businesspeople buy a region, support their franchisees and grow franchisee numbers. Jim has had hundreds of people selling franchises over the years — because *they* wanted to. It wasn't just a job, it was an investment they bought into because they believed in it. This has grown Jim's far bigger than a few salesmen on a salary ever could.

Despite his system's success overall, there are some cases where Jim has needed to step in. Jim recently went to court regarding the Jim's Diggers division, which was written about by Michael Bailey at the *Australian Financial Review*[1] in November 2017. Michael Bailey wrote that the Thorntons, the family that were the divisional and acting regional franchisor for Jim's Diggers, alleged they were 'wrongly issued a breach notice' in March. Someone had 'inquired about a Jim's Diggers franchise' to the 'competing digger hire franchise system' Dial-A-Digger, which the Thorntons established in 1984. This person went on to purchase a Dial-A-Digger franchise, not a Jim's Digger's franchise. Jim issued them a breach notice.

The Thorntons showed the court emails they wrote to National Office indicating their intention to discuss Dial-A-Digger with prospective Jim's Diggers inquiries, and vice versa, alleging the Jim's Group made no objection to it.

The article listed more allegations the Thorntons made, including that the 'Jim's Group then conspired to have JD [Jim's Diggers] Franchising "voted out"' by their franchisors, explaining that the Thorntons felt it 'amounted to unconscionable conduct' and 'breached the Franchising Code of Conduct'.

Deterioration in Diggers

In 2013 there had been problems in the Diggers division, which was run by the Thornton family. (The Thornton family declined to be interviewed for this book.) Paul Sandles explained that the Victorian franchisees were frustrated 'because we had no support... and we didn't have a lot of leads', which are the key reasons people buy a franchise rather than being an independent. Jim called a meeting with the franchisees and the Thorntons in his office, explaining the vote-out process that could be done. The Thorntons agreed to make certain changes and the franchisees agreed to not hold a vote.

But matters did not improve. Paul Sandles joined Jim's Diggers in April 2014, the tenth Diggers franchisee in Victoria, and quickly became aware of the issues. Over the next two months three of the ten franchisees left. They had each invested $70 000 to become a Diggers franchisee but were so disenchanted they walked away from the investment, losing $35 000 after selling their machinery. (Normally franchisees sell their business to exit with at least what they invested, but there weren't enough leads to be able to sell.)

As Paul described it, the Thorntons had hired a manager to support them how a franchisor normally would: doing the proactive calls and running the meetings. 'Though he [the manager] was a lovely guy, he had no excavation or earth moving experience,' Paul said. Lacking proper support, the franchisees banded together and helped one another. 'We worked as a co-op,' Paul explained. 'We had a pretty good group of guys. But there was no support at all. From our perspective, there was no value add from the Thorntons.'

In 2015 things went from bad to worse until four of the remaining seven franchisees were ready to walk. They contacted Jim, who immediately got involved to rectify the issues. Jim called a meeting, and Paul was one of the three franchisees who arrived with no idea what it was about. 'Jim explained we could vote out the Thorntons, but they would not be gone straight away — the Thorntons would have the chance to rectify the issues, as is the process,' Paul said.

Having four franchisees on the verge of leaving was a big concern to the remaining three. Paul explained, 'If you have one franchisee your advertising budget is $300 a month, which is not a lot, but if you have ten it's $3000, which makes a massive difference'. Three wouldn't be enough to keep Jim's Diggers going in Victoria.

Tino Grossi was at the meeting and he suggested Paul step forward as the new franchisor. 'He sort of plucked me out,' said Paul, who hadn't considered this possibility.

Paul bought the franchisor rights in December 2015, nervous that four of his six franchisees were ready to walk. He had a beer with each of them individually, and asked them for a six-month commitment to stay in the business so there was time to turn it around. All four agreed, and Paul immediately set to work.

The Thorntons were still the divisional for Diggers and initially there was 'a lot of head-butting' between Paul and them, Paul said. In 2016 Paul nearly doubled franchisee numbers while tripling the leads, and his franchisees were thrilled. 'Paul's done a very good job with the division,' Jim said. 'He's a good guy, and a good friend.' All of the four who were ready to walk are still in Jim's Diggers today.

Legal challenges

But in early 2017 issues arose again, which is what sparked the legal battle Michael Bailey wrote about in the *Australian Financial Review*[2] in November 2017. Jim found out about the Dial-A-Digger franchisee who had initially inquired about a Jim's Diggers franchise. The Thorntons own the competing earthmoving company known as Dial-A-Digger, but Jim had agreed in their contract that they could operate both, as long as there was no conflict of interest.

Jim sent the Thorntons a breach notice, based on the conflict of interest clause. 'In effect, we told them to sell one business or the other,' Jim said. He said he 'offered them six months to sell their divisional rights, or I would pay $150 000 for them, plus the right to sell certain regional franchises'. Jim claimed the Thorntons refused this and launched a legal challenge, claiming no conflict of interest and getting an injunction to avoid immediate termination.

The hearing between Jim and the Thorntons was held at the Victorian Supreme Court in October 2017. According to the article in the *Australian Financial Review*[3] the Thorntons 'wanted reinstatement of their divisional franchisor contract or damages'.

The mediation went nowhere for several hours, with the parties sitting in separate rooms. Eventually, Jim lost patience. 'I stood up and threatened to walk out unless Dave Thornton and I could meet alone,' Jim said. This was done,

> and fifteen minutes later the case was settled...with the added proviso that they forgive the debts owed by two regional franchisors.

What is interesting about this case is that Jim was making decent money out of the way the Thorntons were running the division. Jim could have turned a blind eye and enjoyed the profits the Thorntons were bringing in, but he did the opposite. Jim said it

> wasn't profitable for us fighting them in court. We were actually making a lot of money out of the Thorntons, but what really got me angry and upset was the way they treated their franchisors and franchisees.

There was one particular case that really made Jim mad. Ryan Hucklebridge was a franchisor-franchisee, and after the Thorntons terminated his franchisor rights, according to Jim, they continued to chase him down for fees. Jim vented angrily,

> The poor guy had to sell his house! Ryan had invested big in this regional business and he lost it. Then they chased him for the fees he owed despite the fact he was broke. It was unconscionable! The poor guy's lost his business, lost his house. They said it was all his fault and tried to terminate him as a franchisee too, but I wouldn't let them, so they sued him for the fees that he owed. That's why I would only settle with the Thorntons under the proviso they stop pursuing Ryan. We also paid off another franchisor's debt and reduced all the fees when we took over the division.

The Thorntons case cost Jim upwards of $300 000 in legal fees and costs to buy back the division, and his income from the division was actually reduced, but he doesn't regret a cent. 'I just can't stand to see people being treated unfairly,' Jim said.

In November 2017 Jim appointed Paul Sandles as the Diggers divisional manager because of his success as franchisor. I asked Paul if he felt supported by Jim, and he replied 'one hundred per cent'. He continued,

> Jim's care level for the franchisees is incredibly high, and his care for franchisors is incredibly high if they are looking after their franchisees. As long as I continue supporting my guys, I'll have 100 per cent of Jim's support.

He paused and added, 'if you do the wrong thing, be prepared for the wrath' like the Thorntons experienced. 'You'll lose your business.' Yet, 'I've never heard him raise his voice.'

I asked if he thinks Jim's actions were fair. He responded,

> He's never taken over divisions that are going well. If you talked to the jaded party they'd say it was completely unfair, and they'll blame Jim. But Jim can't do something that's illegal — we all have contracts, and we have to do the right thing otherwise we can be breached or terminated. Jim's not a bully. He gave the Thorntons every opportunity to work with him, and they refused. They thought it was a witch hunt and approached it that way. I think the Parke brothers who had Skip Bins felt it was a witch hunt as well, but the reality is I don't think it's ever a witch hunt. The contract allows for due process.

Jim still gets upset when he thinks back to this time:

> People have to be treated decently and fairly. I don't get upset at people trying to cheat me, I get upset at them trying to cheat somebody weaker than them. If you talk to the Thorntons, you'll get a litany of woe. 'Poor me! I've been bullied, I've been treated badly.' But if you talk to the people they've hurt, it's a totally different story.

Mental health challenges in the Jim's Group

Over the years Jim has come to more strongly appreciate the importance of mental health. The significance of this came into heartbreaking clarity in September 2018 when a Jim's Mowing franchisee in Western Australia, Anthony Harvey, allegedly killed his wife, three daughters and mother-in-law.

Like many others in the Jim's Group, Jim was shocked and appalled when he learned of this. He flew to Perth for a dedicated meeting with franchisees, asking for ideas on how to make such tragedies less likely in the future. More than a hundred turned up. Several proposals were made, including a fridge magnet to be mailed to each franchisee with mental health support numbers; that each franchisee provide a secondary contact (usually their partner) in case they failed to keep in regular contact; that certain franchisees be trained as mentors to provide support; and that the Jim's Group set up a national counselling service with trained psychologists. At the time of writing, all these approaches are being pursued.

Jim said,

> The obvious lesson was that contact needed to be more intensive and, in particular, more frequent. It also needed to focus more on the personal relationship rather than on giving business advice.

The strength of the relationship between the franchisor and franchisee encourages franchisees to ask for help when needed, whether for personal or business issues. Jim said,

> Anthony had been in the system for three years and shown no sign of trouble, but received only monthly phone calls and not uncommonly

failed to respond. Closer contact might just possibly have picked something up.

As a direct result of the Perth meeting the contracts were changed to require franchisors to contact new franchisees at least weekly, but also, as Jim said,

> requiring them [the franchisees] to respond. Tragedies at this level are rare and perhaps unavoidable, but depression and other mental health issues seem to be a growing problem in the modern world. A franchise system that aims to put franchisees first must do everything possible to respond.

Tino Grossi knows painfully well how important it is to do as much as you can before tragedy happens.

> I'd known my brother was unstable for quite some time ... I'd told him to see a doctor. He said, 'Only weak people need to see doctors,' and I said, 'That's not true,' and he got agitated. A week later, on Boxing Day 2014, my sister called, asking me to drive to our brother's house to check on him. I drove over and ... he had a hose around his neck. He'd hung himself. I was a broken man.

Tino learned an agonising lesson:

> If you know someone is in a bad way, insist they do what you believe they need. Because if I'd done that with my brother ... I could have saved him from dying. But I was inexperienced and worrying about his feelings rather than worrying about his health. I could have been more persistent. I could have not left the house until he'd come with me to a doctor. I honestly think I could have made a difference with him. It's haunted me ever since.

I asked Tino if Anthony Harvey had showed any signs in his work. Tino said,

> No, none whatsoever. We have put a lot of things in place since. We're doing everything we can to make sure we don't leave any stone unturned. We're adding to the contract that we want a second contact for franchisees. And Jim has made fridge magnets for every franchisee…Jim's number is on the fridge magnet as well. I'd never seen Jim in tears before this—he's broken down three times regarding what happened with Anthony.

When I interviewed Paul Sandles he spoke of how important mental health is:

> It's very close to my heart; I've suffered from depression. I am much better now because of being part of the Jim's Group; I think we're much more open about it than other organisations. I always have a mental health element as part of our monthly newsletters and a session on it at every conference.

On top of this, today Jim's research (discussed in the next two chapters) is focused on finding a way to help people suffering with addiction, and he hopes it will help with other mental illnesses as well. It is early days, but Jim said he is 'pouring millions into finding an effective cure'.

18

Funding a Lifelong Passion

For Jim, his research 'was the background behind everything I did, my ultimate purpose behind Jim's Mowing'. Through all the years, Jim never lost sight of his goal: funding his research. And in late 2005 he finally had money to spare. I asked if it was tough having to wait twenty-four years.

'I thought about it every day,' he replied simply. Since then Jim has spent several million dollars conducting studies that have helped develop his theory of what makes civilisations rise and fall, with exciting discoveries that could help improve mental health.

Jim's theory, summarised

His basic idea is that human societies, and all of human history, can be best understood in terms of evolutionary biology. To explain it, Jim first decribed 'slow' and 'fast' life history strategy as follows.

Slow life history strategy

Animals in a limited-food environment have to plan for the future by searching out food supplies even when not hungry (the animal equivalent of 'work'). They must drive away competitors for food, and with less food available they become less social, at the extreme defending an exclusive territory. Another way of looking at this is they become more 'impersonal' in their attitudes, oriented to defending a piece of land rather than bonding with other animals.

They do not tend to breed until they have secured territory, because without it they would have little chance of successfully raising young, and when young are born they spend a great deal of effort raising them. In this ultra-competitive environment, only the fittest have a chance to breed. Gibbons are a classic example of slow life history strategy, living in the jungles of South-East Asia where food supplies are steady but strictly limited. Gibbons are genetically programmed with these attitudes, but most animals only show them when food is limited.

Evolutionary psychologists describe this behaviour as a 'slow life history strategy' because it looks to the future rather than to immediate gratification.

Fast life history strategy

By contrast, baboons show a 'fast life history strategy'. They mate often and young, and do not search for food unless hungry. They are also relatively tolerant of other baboons, showing a more 'personal' orientation than gibbons. The young are weaned early and left to fend for themselves. This short-term thinking and focus on immediate gratification is a proper response to a dangerous world where predation, rather than food shortage, is the main danger. Success in life, which in evolutionary terms means carrying genes to the next generation, is best achieved by bonding with others and breeding fast and early.

High C and high V behaviour

According to Jim, it so happens that 'slow life history' behaviour is exactly what civilisation needs. Farming depends on working now for future benefit. Business success, and investing in education and advanced technical skills, requires a more extreme form of the same attitude. Having a more impersonal orientation helps people bond to a more distant political leader, or, at the more extreme level, to a nation or code of laws. Societies that show such behaviour tend to outcompete those that do not. Jim calls this strategy 'high C', because it is characteristic of civilisation.

Crucially, Jim's theory states that this high C behaviour is not just triggered by food shortage, but can also be promoted by culturally driven behaviours, such as chastity, that are embedded in major religions. In other words, the theory is that humans unwittingly triggered this biological mechanism, evolved for one purpose, for a very different purpose.

'There is no "right" strategy, both a fast and slow life history strategy are useful in their correct contexts,' Jim explained.

> The problem is that many humans have a fast life history strategy but live in a society where a slow life history strategy would work better. You are more likely to have a prosperous life if you stay home and study, rather than go out and take drugs.

The behaviours of 'high C' finally answered Jim's lifelong question of why Ancient Rome collapsed.

By becoming overly wealthy they gradually lost the high C character that had made them successful in the first place, and the same thing is happening in our own time. Effects include stagnating wages, loss of faith in democratic government, rising levels of drug addiction and an epidemic of mental illness. These problems are likely to become much worse in the future.

Andrew Penman, Jim's son, explained,

Part of Jim's theory is that governments largely reflect the temperament and character of their people, so if the temperament of the people changes on a deep neurological level, the government and society will change too. Everything from the desire to reproduce, to fight off invaders, and even second-generation effects that are specific to humans such as the attitudes towards representative government and the economy, can potentially be understood in terms of evolutionary psychology and neuroscience.

Jim realised there was also another part of the puzzle: vigour (V). He describes this as an evolved reaction to occasional but severe stresses, such as famine and predator attack. The effect makes animals far more aggressive, but also more able to bond for small group defence. The classic example, again, is the savannah baboon, living in an environment with fierce predators such as lions and leopards, and with occasional famines. V allows baboons to band together to fight off predators (a baboon troop can mob and even kill a full-grown leopard). It also lets them migrate long distances when local food supplies disappear, making them better able to cope with drought.

In human societies V is associated with warfare, which is why bands from harsh environments, such as mountains and deserts, commonly invade and settle civilised lands. Settled life, being safer and less prone to famine, tends to undermine V, but a society that can maintain V has an advantage over one that does not. As Jim explained,

> Very low levels of V have undesirable effects such as low morale, lesser resistance to disease, and it seems to undermine C. Declining C and V reduce interest in children and thus lead to shrinking, ageing populations.

Jim is also very interested in drug and alcohol addiction, which he sees as the result of fast life history strategy attitudes (low C).

> If you're very short-term in your thinking, you might shoot up with heroin. If you're longer term, you think, 'Hang on a minute, if I shoot up I'll feel good now, but tomorrow I'll feel terrible. It'll also mean I've committed a crime, so I might go to jail. I might have an infected needle. I might get AIDS'. Having a slow life history strategy means you can assess those risks and decide 'I'm not going to do that'.

The crucial discovery from the research conducted thus far is that it may not be difficult to shift someone in the direction of a slow life history strategy. Jim said,

> One crucial finding from our research is that our neurology can be switched from fast to slow life history strategies (or the reverse) by pheromones. These are natural substances already present in our social environment, including family and friends, which greatly influence our physiology and behaviour. Children brought up by fast life history strategy parents, and with peers of the same nature, will themselves tend to show fast life history strategy behaviour. This means, for example, they are more likely to be impulsive or violent, take drugs or drop out of school. But if we can identify

the pheromones involved we could potentially negate this, helping them to live productive and healthier lives. That is what excites me the most.

Jim and THE VALUE OF WORK

Jim believes work is essential to the character of a person:

What is the worst thing you can do to undermine character and cause people to fail in life? Give them money for not working. The worst thing about welfare is the effect it has on those who get the money. Every study shows that people who don't work are more depressed, have more substance abuse, et cetera. Even if you have the same income, you're worse off if you don't work. The whole notion of giving people money for not working, unless somebody's really, obviously sick and needs support, is bad. Welfare is destructive because work creates character and welfare undermines it.

Coming to his theory

Having money for research in 2005 was one thing — spending it proved more difficult. Jim first employed a Monash University graduate to do literature research, 'but that went nowhere,' he said. While discussing this with academics at Monash they suggested he find someone already working in the field, 'which was extremely good advice,' Jim said, and he immediately started looking.

One night in 2005 Tony Paolini, an assistant professor at La Trobe University, was in his study checking his emails. He saw one offering half a million dollars for research over the next few years, which looked like spam, and he was about to click 'delete' when he thought, 'What if it's not?' So instead he googled this 'Jim Penman' who had sent the email, and discovered he was a La Trobe University alumnus and the founder of the Jim's Group. He replied instantly. Steve Kent, also working at La Trobe at that time, received the same email and also responded.

Jim's first donation was $500 000 (he has given millions to his research since). In 2006 Rachel Gibson published an article about Jim's research in *The Age*, writing at the time that Jim 'hopes the research might one day lead to a cure for a range of social ills, including obesity, drug addiction, child neglect and even economic backwardness.'

Early results

Tony and Steve set about conducting the studies. There was already research indicating mild calorie restriction is beneficial for health, 'but Jim wanted to take a different look,' Tony explained. 'He wanted to look at what other effects it has on psychological behaviour.'

They investigated the effects mild calorie restriction in rats had on behaviours such as exploration, response to strangers, sexual behaviour, maternal behaviour and anxiety. And they 'looked at how this differs depending on the stage of development,' Tony said. For example, Jim wanted to know the effects of calorie restriction when experienced by the mother before conception, during gestation and while nursing. They found the effects could differ quite widely.

Jim funded La Trobe University PhD scholarships for Antonina Govic and Elizabeth Levay, who worked with Tony and Steve on the research. Over the next few years Jim funded more PhD students. Steve Kent said,

Unlike many people he puts his money where his mouth is, funding projects that will investigate the theory without favour. He accepts the data: if it works great, if it doesn't it's annoying and disappointing but it is what it is.

Jim would analyse the results with the researchers every few months, 'and he'd incorporate the findings to develop and correct his ideas,' Tony said.

Jim was and is absolutely thrilled with the research: 'It radically changed my theory'.

Developing his theory

The following years saw more money given, more research done, and Jim continued developing his theory. A major contribution from Tony was the idea that epigenetics, a new field of science looking at how environment makes certain genes more or less active, must be involved. This was not mainstream science when Jim completed his PhD in the 1970s, but it later explained a great deal that had puzzled him at the time. Tony investigated, and found that food restriction caused a number of significant epigenetic changes.

Published results[2] helped in getting grants from the Australian Research Council to explore mild calorie restriction further. Until 2008 there was also a partnership with the Bionics Institute at Melbourne's St Vincent's Hospital.

The results showed that a mild calorie restricted diet brought clear benefits, particularly reduced anxiety. In 2008–09 they began exploring if it could be possible for humans to gain these benefits *without* restricting their diet. 'We thought there must be some sensory cue that helps bind behaviours in a group of animals, or even in a human population,' Tony said.

Jim suggested it could be pheromones, and they tested this theory by exposing a group of rats to the bedding of other rats that had been mildly calorie restricted. 'We wanted to see whether their behaviour would change in a similar way to the calorie-restricted animals', even though they had not been mildly calorie restricted themselves,' Tony said. This was done in a controlled experiment, comparing their behaviour with that of rats getting the bedding from fully fed rats.

For Jim this was a real nail-biter. (He actually does bite his nails, a habit from childhood he hasn't been able to shake.) 'I expected some effect but didn't know how strong it would be. I knew it might not even be statistically significant,' Jim said. But the results were astonishing, 'beyond my wildest hopes!' Jim exclaimed. The rats exposed to the bedding of calorie-restricted animals showed the same behaviour as those that had been calorie restricted, to roughly the same extent. The implications of this, 'from rebalancing natural human pheromones in struggling parents, to improving concentration in students and treating addictions, is immense,' Jim said.

There is still a long way to go before any of this comes to fruition. The first step is finding out which of the thousands of compounds in the calorie-restricted rats' urine is having this effect, and then further extensive testing needs to be done before beginning human trials. 'So far we've only scratched the surface,' Tony said.

The research continues today. Antonina Govic, who is still part of the team, said,

I'm trying to look at behavioural changes, applying them to mental illnesses like anxiety, depression and even aggressive behaviour. The good thing about the theory is it crosses many disciplines. It's very complex and there's so much to learn, but it's all testable.

I asked Tony what it's like working with Jim. 'I think you see the real Jim when you hear him talk about his research. He has such passion for it,' Tony said, 'when he gets excited he gets really animated'. Steve Kent said,

Jim is incredibly passionate when he talks about his theory. He's clearly driven, and is more likely to achieve goals because he's going to push until he does. And that's incredibly commendable, even inspirational.

Jim's children have been brought up with his unique ideas. His son Andrew, now thirty-two, is the most interested in Jim's theory. What began as father–son discussions by the barbecue has evolved into a partnership of two adults hugely passionate about these ideas. 'Andrew became the first person apart from myself to understand the potential of behavioural epigenetics in understanding social and historical change,' Jim said. 'It's really an amazing thing to have one of your kids understand the basic premise and see how it's a clue to what's going wrong with society and what could be done to change it!'

Funding an obsession

Many millionaires spend their money on fancy cars, big boats, exotic holidays, and so on. Jim does not. For many years, after his original beat-up Kingswood gave up the ghost, he drove a beat up, thirty-year-old yellow Volvo. Jill Stallworthy remembers him coming into work one Monday saying his Volvo had failed on the weekend, but he was able to find another just like it for '$500!' Today, he drives a six-year-old Mitsubishi.

When Li and Jim married, she furnished the house with all of her own furniture because Jim didn't have much, nor an inclination to buy any. If you walked past Jim on the street you'd have no idea he is wealthy. His house is on a 5-acre block in Mooroolbark and would have cost more than most can afford, but the house itself gives no sign of grandeur. My middle-class roots made me feel more at home in his house than in some of his franchisees' and franchisors' homes.

Where Jim does spend — besides his investment properties and his farm in Don Valley — is in business. He happily experiments with different business ideas, like he did with BarterBank and his Marysville resort project in the 1990s and, more recently, with his other trade exchange, TradeNet. From the outside his spending on business experiments seems excessive, but to him it is anything but. Jim said,

> If I spend $100 000 on ten different ideas, and just one turns into a multimillion-dollar venture, it is well worth the risk and expense of the nine that failed.

In the day-to-day running of the business Jim is frugal; you need only see his offices to see that. He runs the Jim's Group like a lean start-up, with only forty staff at National Office.

But his top priority will always be the research project. He has given many millions to it over the years.

> I want to make the world a better place, to help find cures for addiction and depression and other ills. I also want it to be a better world for my kids to grow up in. Nothing is more important than that.

19

It's All About Character

In 2012, after continually developing his theory for forty-one years, it was time for Jim to start the mammoth task of writing his theory in an academic book. In January of that year Jim hired his son Andrew to do research and be a technical assistant for the project. Jim, meanwhile, set aside time each day to write.

Jim is very grateful for Andrew's interest:

I used to be terrified that if I died all my research would go to nothing. So when Andrew became interested it was wonderful, a miracle. He's very bright and dedicated. We have our disagreements, but he's amazing. It's one of my greatest blessings, having a son like him.

After two years of labour the manuscript was complete. Andrew suggested calling the theory 'Biohistory', which became the book's title. It is 622 pages long with extensive footnotes, appropriate for an academic audience but not the general public, who wouldn't want to read *quite* that much detail. So, a year later, a shorter, more accessible version was finished. They gave it the title *Biohistory: Decline and fall of the West*, since one of its key conclusions is that Western civilisation, like Ancient Rome, will inevitably decline unless a better understanding of the neurophysiological basis of social change can stop it.

Both versions of *Biohistory* were published in March 2015, and are currently available on Amazon and from the website www.biohistory.org.

Andrew said the book,

> In its broad outline, gives a sophisticated reason as to why societies collapse — the character of the population changes on a deep neurological level as a direct response to the very act of living in an urban environment, making the society unviable — it gives a road map to understanding social collapse on a biological basis.

He continued,

> A history professor who worked with us on some sections of the book said it was hands down the best grand historical theory he had ever come across ... [But] the main issue with the book is that it claims to be fully scientific, when in reality it is grounded in the humanities. Jim does not have a background in psychology, neuroscience, zoology or evolutionary ecology. He has a PhD in history and cross-cultural anthropology.

Andrew is completing a degree in neuroscience and aims to explore potential links between behavioural epigenetics and social psychology.

Jim agreed that

> Andrew is right that we need to engage with the scientific community. In particular, we must develop effective treatments for

mental health problems, which I'm quite confident we can do. Then people will be likely to take us more seriously. So for the moment, our focus is on the scientific work.

Jim has organised his family trust so that if something happens to him there's enough to support his family, but all the funds from his business would go to support the research, which Andrew is in charge of.

Jim's University?

One venture in particular has the potential to kick the research to a much higher level. In 2013 Tony Paolini, who was carrying out Jim's research at La Trobe, was appointed professor at RMIT University in Melbourne, and became Head of Psychology two years later. Jim's research project went with him, 'which was great because they had really good-quality labs,' Tony said. In late 2014 Tony and Jim began discussing ways to promote the study of evolutionary psychology, which encapsulates Jim's research, to grow the field and get students interested in it.

In 2015 Jim and Tony explored starting an institute with a focus on evolutionary psychology. This would mean they could educate students themselves, 'teaching a unified theory of psychology,' Tony said.

They are the co-owners of what is now called the Institute for Social Neuroscience (ISN), with Jim as director and Tony the president. Jim provides the funding, Tony the sweat equity and Steve Kent, the other original researcher, is on the academic board. Tony said,

I think Jim was apprehensive about whether we would get students, but I felt confident that ISN Psychology would be new and different, and fit perfectly with what Jim needed.

Their focus is on placements for masters students, the key qualifications needed to practise as a psychologist. Universities typically have large numbers of Psychology undergraduate students, since they are more cost effective to teach, but too few placements for higher degrees.

The process to apply for Tertiary Education Quality and Standards Agency (TEQSA) approval took longer and cost far more than expected, and it was a lot of work to set up all the procedures and policies, but Tony managed to navigate it. 'There were times that I regretted the whole venture, because we were so tight for money,' Jim said. Their first premises, on Martin Street in Heidelberg, though run as a clinic, did not nearly cover the rental and staff costs.

On Christmas Eve 2016, while they were still waiting for TEQSA approval, Tony noticed a large building was to be constructed in Ivanhoe, not far from their clinic. A large section of the ground floor was available, so he called Jim. 'If we want to expand, this would be perfect,' Tony said.

Despite it being Christmas Eve, they called the agent and Jim decided to buy it.

In February 2017 they received TEQSA approval and began accepting students, but numbers were limited because they were new and did not qualify for the government's FEE-HELP system until June 2018. Antonina Govic, one of the first two PhD students Jim funded, who has worked closely on Jim's research since, today works at ISN. 'It's really an exciting time, I feel like I'm part of something big and important, which is really motivating,' Antonina said.

In early 2018 Tony left RMIT to work at ISN Psychology full time. Student numbers expanded and Jim awarded his first batch of grants for research, mostly to ISN staff, with the students heavily involved. According to its website,

> The Institute for Social Neuroscience aims to investigate the basis of character and temperament through the study of psychology, epigenetics, biochemistry, neuroscience and ecology and to apply these findings to improving the health of individuals and societies.

'Our institute provides the basis to really understand human nature,' Tony said.

> I don't think there is anything out there that is so driven to educate students about what underpins human nature; what are we all about, what drives us and how that drive will change in a changing world.

For Jim, the central purpose of ISN has always been to further his research goals.

'It's been a great advantage having in-house staff committed to evolutionary biology, with most of them running biohistory-related projects,' Jim said. 'Universities are become increasingly rigid in their thinking, and we want to provide a real alternative, training students to think for themselves.'

Character

Jim's research has greatly influenced how he looks at the world. It has influenced his values, his daily habits and how he runs the Jim's Group. It affects which political party he votes for, what school he sends his children to and how he hopes our civilisation will move forward—though he fears it will not.

My observation is that at any moment Jim will be engaged in one of the following activities: working on his business, spending time with his children, working in the garden, reading or having lunch with his wife.

Jim's values are traditional. He mentioned to me that he did an online survey to find out which historical era he should have lived in. His result was, unsurprisingly, the Victorian Era.

'In those days people were judged by temperament more than personality. I would have done much better then,' Jim mused.

People were judged by their morals and principles instead of how charming they were. Even a small example — people back then didn't smile in photos.

Even so, he defies easy categorisation. He personally loathes abortion but would not ban it. He got into trouble at his very traditional high school for publicly supporting gay rights. (Both his fourteen-year-old and sixteen-year-old daughters, Esther and Sylvia, are quite left wing. Esther said, 'I used to think that he's sexist and homophobic because I didn't talk to him about it, but when I did, he's actually very accepting'.) Today he is against any sexual relationship outside of marriage, though he admitted it can be 'very, very hard to live such a lifestyle'. He rigorously avoids addictive substances (alcohol, cigarettes, drugs, coffee) but would make any and all drugs legal. ('Illegality causes far more harm than is justified by reduced usage, if there is any.') He eats a mainly vegetarian diet, but for health and taste rather than principle. He attends a fundamentalist church each Sunday and sends his children to the associated school, but is a fervent evolutionist. He sees global warming as a serious danger and would support a 'sky-high' carbon tax, but strongly opposes Green policies such as zoning restrictions and solar power rebates, which he sees as enriching elites at the expense of ordinary people. He dislikes big government but supports policies such as property tax, which could narrow the gap between rich and poor. He reveres the military but hates war.

Jim is deeply religious and hosts a Bible study group each week, something he began in 2014. I interviewed numerous friends from the group and gleaned insight into a different side of Jim. All remarked on his generosity.

Eric Skattebo spoke of Jim's generosity as a friend, and how much they enjoy long conversations about history. Eric and his son enjoy playing laser tag with Jim and his kids, though they are usually beaten (Jim and his children love laser tag, and have become skilled).

Tom Winter said he 'hadn't found Jim to be like the stories; I've found him quite generous and kind'. When the group were meeting at Jim's house he would pay for takeaway dinner for everyone, and now that they meet at Foothills Jim provides them all with dinner prepared by his chef.

Brian Johnson only realised Jim is 'the Jim' the third time he attended the group. His first impression of Jim was

> truly, quite ordinary. I say that in a respectful way. I thought he was open and hospitable, always making sure everyone was fed, though with no fanfare, he was very matter of fact in his generosity.

Brian suffers bad migraines, and said out of everyone in the group, Jim is one of the few who consistently and regularly calls him to ask how he's doing. 'When someone rings and takes a genuine interest in you, it makes a difference. Jim does, regularly.'

As time has gone on, the group has become more open and vulnerable with each other, Jim included. 'Jim will give you space to express yourself; he's very honest about his own character,' Brian said. He added that Jim is very open about his character flaws in the group, and talks with them about how he wants to control his anger. 'He's very self-aware, and not afraid to challenge himself,' Brian said.

In his working life Jim is a zealot for looking after franchisees as a group, yet that can mean forcing out an individual franchisee who has received too many complaints and is tarnishing the brand. He despises the unfairness and inequality of the legal system, yet uses it to his advantage with every single legal battle. He is exceptionally frugal with his personal expenses, but is happy to spend hundreds of thousands to further the business and millions on his research.

The one constant is his lack of emotional reactions to things that would affect most people. If someone doesn't like him, he doesn't seem to care. Even if he has years of history with that person. He moves on quickly, and will often still talk well of them despite what transpired. If a business experiment turns south, losing him a lot of money, he doesn't get upset — he instantly, rationally wonders why it went wrong and what can be done better next time.

When he hears that a past franchisor or divisional has initiated legal action against him, he feels no emotional anguish over the broken-down relationship, nor the money he'll have to spend on lawyers. This comes across as cold, calculating and unfeeling.

Yet Jim is extremely passionate about the welfare of everyone in Jim's. He genuinely wants others to succeed, and when he hears of a past Jim's person who has left and started their own successful business, he feels nothing but happiness and pride for them.

Multiple people commented to me that Jim could have Asperger's or be on the spectrum, though he has never been tested. His son Andrew said,

> People like Jim, like Elon Musk, who are very successful, do have these characteristics. I don't think you would classify Jim as having autism spectrum disorder, but he has traits that you might associate with autism.

Perhaps it is best to say that Jim seems to have a character profile that has traits you can find in some other very successful businesspeople — an intense ability to focus, a disregard for small talk, an emotional disconnect and a passion for doing a job right and building something great above all else.

Yet Jim sees his failures in character as a reason he has not done a great deal better.

> The fact is I'm not as hardworking or as disciplined as I should be. I really envy people like my daughter Jasmine or son Richard, who are so hardworking by nature. If I was like them I could have achieved so much more. I waste at least an hour a day playing computer games. I read the paper in the evening when I should be working. I love foods like pizza and chocolate and it's a struggle not to put on weight… It's a terrible betrayal when I've been given so much that I haven't achieved a great deal more.

One particular weakness is his inability to get involved in an aspect of the business thoroughly, to understand and fix it. 'Li does it so well. Not being able to do that has cost me a *lot*.'

Still, Jim has been able to build what is arguably Australia's largest franchise. At sixty-six he still works every day, passionate about keeping his company on course.

Jim and EXERCISE

Exercise is an important part of Jim's daily routine. Ever since his late twenties, when he got into terrible debt because all he did was read on his beanbag, he has made it a top priority. 'Without exercise I am very lazy,' Jim said.

I've read all the recent studies that show, again and again, that exercise makes you more efficient at work, it improves your mood, and it's far better than any antidepressant on the market. It's a wonderful cure-all! If you could put the benefits of exercise into a pill it'd be worth trillions of dollars. But you've got to get out there and do it, and the discipline is not always easy.

How much does Jim exercise?

The basic guideline is half an hour of vigorous exercise a day, something that roughly doubles your pulse rate. So I normally run five kilometres on a treadmill, unless I'm doing gardening, which is often for hours on end. I walk wherever I can. I live next to National Office so I walk there and back several times a day I walk around the office, I don't like sitting at my desk talking to people, I usually go to them. I always take stairs if possible, instead of lifts or escalators.

Jim said exercise makes his mind clearer and his work more efficient, and, for a man of sixty-six, his energy levels are incredible. 'I don't feel, think or act my age,' Jim said.

I've got this strong sense of drive and passion which hasn't faded one bit. Being fit has a lot to do with that. People my age who don't exercise and get overweight lose their edge. If I didn't run I'd feel guilty. Getting on the treadmill in the morning is just a part of my life, like having breakfast (which is almost always oatmeal).

Jim is also a strong believer in cold showers, even in the middle of winter.

Cold water is what's called a 'eustress' or good stress, because it gives the stress reaction system a sharp workout to make it function better. There's a lot of literature on cold water as a treatment for depression, and I find it builds energy and resilience. And it's really not that hard to get used to, especially when you're hot from a run.

20

Looking to the Future

After the wild journey of the past forty-eight years in business, a different person might look at this as a time to sit back and rest on their laurels. But that's just not Jim's nature. He's still using his abilities as a big-picture, long-term thinker to look to the future. Not only has he spent enormous effort thinking about how society was thousands of years ago, and what it might be far into the future, he also directs his long-term thinking to his business. Cynthia Tjong, the head of finance, explained, 'His vision is long term. He doesn't focus on what we're doing now'.

Tino Grossi shared the same sentiment: 'Jim can see what people will want in the future, what the needs of the country will be, and not in one month, not in the near future — he sees the far future'.

Ben Siddons, a divisional manager, said, 'He's very, very strategic. He's always thinking, always has ideas'.

Perhaps the best example of Jim's ability to think into the future is his latest business venture, an aggregator site called GoBlitz. Aggregators are typically websites that aggregate related and frequently updated content from various sources for easy viewing in one consolidated place. Examples for booking a flight are Webjet and Skyscanner, which search for the cheapest fares on multiple websites and aggregate that information onto one webpage for you. In the home service industry, websites like hipages and Airtasker are Jim's competition — they aggregate a wide range of home-service providers that can be booked online.

In 1989 when Jim's began, the only way to have your lawn mowed was to call, but today Millennials prefer booking online; it's quick, easy and they can assess the reviews. In 2016 Jim saw the big threat aggregator sites pose to his franchise, and began thinking of ways to stay relevant. The issue Jim saw with hipages, Airtasker, and other such sites is they force contractors to compete on price, and don't have a good way of ensuring the operator will provide great-quality service to the customer.

There has also been another problem on Jim's mind for the past few years — what to do with the 180 000 unserviced leads a year? Jim's call centre staff tell one in four callers, 'Sorry, we don't have an operator in your area currently available.'

'This is not a good experience for our customers, who can get frustrated when they can't get a Jim's person,' Jim said.

Jim believes GoBlitz can be a solution to both problems. It's a website for finding and booking home-service providers — but it's not being launched on its own. Jim funnels the unserviced leads to the site, so customers are given an alternative when no Jim's franchisees are available.

The key difference from other sites is that it looks first to the interest of the contractors, as Jim's does for franchisees, by only allowing customers to book one contractor at a time. With a rigorous survey system it is designed to attract customers who want quality service, rather than the cheapest price, 'which should in turn make it attractive to the best contractors,' Jim said. If GoBlitz takes off, it could potentially revolutionise the home-service industry.

At the franchisor national conference in July 2018, it was the main topic discussed at the general business session. Franchisors voiced their varied concerns about how GoBlitz will affect their businesses, which Jim answered and explained. Jim also made it clear that over the next ten to twenty years, aggregators could put the whole Jim's franchise out of business, reasoning, 'It's better to own our competition than be beaten by them'. You could feel a shift in the room as many realised this. During the discussion a franchisor said, 'so with GoBlitz we're controlling the work we normally just lose anyway — great! We shouldn't be worried at all'.

This is the genius of the idea: not only does it solve current problems that customers, independents, Jim's franchisors and Jim's franchisees face — it means Jim owns at least some of the future competition to his franchise, rather than being destroyed by it.

'Jim has a vision not of today, but of ten years [from now],' Tino said.

> People get upset with his decisions today, but things he decided three years ago that they didn't like, they've embraced today. They say, 'Thank God we're doing this'. Jim's constantly fighting because they don't realise he's *helping* them — he can see further ahead than we can.

But of all his accomplishments, and all his passions, his greatest is his family.

I asked Li, Jim's wife of seventeen years, how she would sum up Jim.

He's actually very generous. He's very keen to learn and grow from his mistakes. He's persistent... He never gives up. He never gets discouraged.

He's a very powerful force; if he wants to go in a direction, he will go no matter what's in the way. I find that amazing.

Sarah Penman, Jim's twenty-eight-year-old daughter, said,

there is a lot of hate out there for Dad and I think that people don't realise that he is not trying to hurt people. He is just a bit of a singularity... he has a goal and everything else falls away from that goal. It's not malicious.

When I sat down to interview Sylvia, his sixteen-year-old daughter, and said I was writing his biography, she replied,

I didn't know Dad was famous enough to get a biography. Wow, that's so cool...

I think everyone would agree, he's kind of awkward, he's a strange person. I guess anyone that's successful is strange. And he's utterly forward about his views, which he also brought in us.

Sylvia mentioned he still does the same dance move Sarah told me about to embarrass them in public.

Well he doesn't really dance; he more just moves, like waves his body and clicks his fingers — it's so weird. My friends found out who he is and said, 'He's a national treasure'. It's weird for me to hear that, because he doesn't strike me as someone who's a national treasure. He's just a weirdo.

Jim is a man who arouses strong emotions, both positive and negative. Few people are neutral about him. He can be very hard on people and seemingly careless of their feelings, yet he is deeply compassionate for those he cares about. He is intensely ambitious but also idealistic, wanting to change the world in fundamental ways.

Perhaps his own unusual character has informed his belief that character is the key to history, to society, to the very future of mankind.

It's ultimately a hopeful philosophy. As Sylvia said of her father,

Dad's lazy, but he changed himself to be hardworking. I think that's really cool. Your success is not dependent on who you are but on what you try to be.

Endnotes

Introduction: 'The Real Jim'

1 Michael Bailey, 14 November 2017. 'Jim's Group mows short court battle with digger franchisor'. *Australian Financial Review.*

Chapter 2: The Accidental Gardener

1 The London School of Economics and Political Science, 13 December 2016. 'Relationships and good health the key to happiness, not income'.

Chapter 4: This Little, Short-term Mowing Business

1 *New Straits Times,* 27 August 1990. 'Canberra Buys State Bank of Victoria'.

Chapter 14: Revolt in the Ranks

1 Chalpat Sonti, 20 October 2009. 'Turfed out: Jim's Mowing magnate faces the sack'. *The Sydney Morning Herald*.

2 Chalpat Sonti, 31 March 2010. 'Jim's Group chief sued'. *The Sydney Morning Herald*.

3 InvestSMART, 31 March 2010. 'Jim's Group chief being sued for $5m by former master franchisee'. investsmart.com.au.

Chapter 17: Duelling Diggers

1 Michael Bailey, 14 November 2017. 'Jim's Group mows short court battle with digger franchisor'. *Australian Financial Review*.

2 ibid.

3 ibid.

Chapter 18: Funding a Lifelong Passion

1 Rachel Gibson, 16 September 2016. 'Weird science or the Jim workout our bodies need?' *The Age*.

2 'The Research'. 2018. Biohistory. https://www.biohistory .org/the-research/.

About the Author

Catherine Moolenschot is a novelist, biographer, public speaker and book writing mentor.

At 13, she wrote her first novel, *A Rough Road*, telling the story a refugee's journey from Africa to Australia. Her latest novel, a coming-of-age story titled *I Am Megan*, was released in June 2018.

She regularly speaks on the Australian and international stage with her successful TEDx talks, 'Living Your Funnel of Greatness' and 'What is the point, really?' making her a go-to presenter for corporate and educational audiences. With her passion for great books that inspire, educate and entertain, Catherine mentors CEOs and professionals through the process of writing their own books. She also ghostwrites, enjoying the process of taking someone's stories and/or content and crafting their book for them.

Catherine lives in Melbourne with her partner David Pagotto.

Learn more at catherinemoolenschot.com

Acknowledgements

Thank you to everyone I interviewed — this book would not exist without you. Your generosity of time, memories, and hunting down facts, such as exactly what date you began with Jim's, was incredible. And to those interviewees who went above and beyond, you know who you are, my sincerest thanks.

Thank you to Jim for letting me research your life to such depth.

A big thanks to my partner, Dave, for your constant support and love.

To my parents and sister for their unwavering support and excitement as I worked on this book.

And thank you to the team at Wiley whose expertise and dedication brought this book into readers' hands.

List of Interviewees

I conducted over one hundred formal interviews in 2018 to write Jim's biography, and had countless informal conversations with people who had worked for Jim, been a franchisee, or had other business dealings with him.

Some interviewees asked not to be mentioned. Here is a list of everyone I formally interviewed who were happy to be named.

Leonard Abiero	Leah Cadwallader	Katherine Doe
Brett Ardley	Glenn Camilleri	George Donopolous
Melissa Avery	Andrew Clerihew	David Douglass
Joe Badr	Paul Commerford	Shane Foran
Prathamesh Bhoir	Sharon Connell	Tony Gale
Brett Blair	Damon Currie	Antonina Govic
Shannon Bridger	Craig Daniel	Tino Grossi
Charlie Bush	Felicity Daniel	Peter Hansen
Jamie Byard	Mike Davenport	Shirley Harry

Jim's Book

Noel Healy

Brendan Hill

Archie Hood

Haydar Hussein

Jason Jaap

Paul Jabke

Matthew James

Brian Johnson

Steve Kent

Matt Lannigan

Meg Leaney

Stuart Lewien

Garry Lewis

Valerie Lobo

Richard Long

Natalie Manning

Phil Maunder

Harley McKean

Trish Mewett

Andrew Michelmore

Gill Moxham

Stewart Nieman

Ali Olmez

Peter Panagiotopoulos

Tony Paolini

Andrew Parke

Craig Parke

Vanessa Parke

Andrew Penman

Esther Penman

Jim Penman

Li Penman

Sarah Penman

Sylvia Penman

Jyosh Polea-Vizcarra

David Pollard

Craig Pritchard

Greg Puzzolo

Eugene Renehan

Tim Respondek

Chris Reyes

Ron Sadowski

Paul Sandles

Jadran Sango

Cameron Scott

Nick Shearme

Jolyon Shelton

Ben Siddons

Anthony Silverman

Eric Skattebo

Jill Stallworthy

Cynthia Tjong

Gary Turton

Silvia Valeri

Barry Walker

Benn Ward

Neil Welsh

Tom Winter

Nicole Wood

Index

Throughout this index, the prefix 'Jim's' for divisions of the Jim's Group business, has been placed second in the index headwords, except for Jim's Group: for example, 'Jim's Mowing' appears as 'Mowing, Jim's'. To clearly distinguish the business from the man, 'Jim' and 'Jim's' refers to the business names of Jim's Group, and 'DJP' represents David James (Jim) Penman throughout.